Appraising and Using Social Research in the Human Services

of related interest

Prevention and Coping in Child and Family Care
Mothers in Adversity Coping with Child Care
Michael Sheppard with Mirka Gröhn
ISBN 1 84310 193 9

Handbook of Theory for Practice Teachers in Social Work
Edited by Joyce Lishman
ISBN 1 85302 098 2

Competence in Social Work Practice
A Practical Guide for Professionals
Edited by Kieran O'Hagan
ISBN 1 85302 332 9

Integrating Theory and Practice in Social Work Education
Florence Watson, Helen Burrows and Chris Player
With contributions from Lorraine Agu, Simon Shreeve and Lee Durrant
ISBN 1 85302 981 5

Social Work and Evidence-Based Practice
Edited by David Smith
ISBN 1 84310 156 4
Research Highlights in Social Work 45

Research in Social Care and Social Welfare
Issues and Debates for Practice
Edited by Beth Humphries
ISBN 1 85302 900 9

User Involvement and Participation in Social Care
Research Informing Practice
Edited by Hazel Kemshall and Rosemary Littlechild
ISBN 1 85302 777 4

Appraising and Using Social Research in the Human Services

An Introduction for Social Work and Health Professionals

Michael Sheppard

Jessica Kingsley Publishers
London and Philadelphia

First published in 2004
by Jessica Kingsley Publishers
116 Pentonville Road
London N1 9JB, UK
and
400 Market Street, Suite 400
Philadelphia, PA 19106, USA

www.jkp.com

Second impression 2005

Library of Congress Cataloging in Publication Data
Sheppard, Michael.
Appraising and using social research in the human services : an introduction for social work
and health professionals / Michael Sheppard.
p. cm.
Includes bibliographical references and index.
ISBN 1-84310–289-7 (pbk.)
1. Human services--Research--Methodology. 2. Social service--Research--Methodology.
3. Evaluation research (Social action programs) I. Title.
HV11.S484 2004
361'.0072--dc22

2004010448

British Library Cataloguing in Publication Data
A CIP catalogue record for this book is available from the British Library

ISBN-13: 978 1 84310 289 2
ISBN-10: 1 84310 289 7

Printed and Bound in Great Britain by
Athenaeum Press, Gateshead, Tyne and Wear

Contents

Preface

The Social Care Institute for Excellence, empowered by government (in the United Kingdom) to disseminate knowledge across the range of social care, has emphasized the importance of 'evidence based practice, with its emphasis on all research users being able to judge the quality of a piece of research' (SCIE 2003, p.60). They comment also (on the same page) that 'critical appraisal [of research] is now routinely taught within academic settings at undergraduate and postgraduate level, and is likely to become a core competency within continuing professional development and elsewhere'. The importance of 'research mindedness', of the capacity to appraise critically relevant research and to incorporate research within practice and practice developments, could hardly have been more strongly stated. This is an area of huge importance, as much to health as social care workers.

This is a book aimed at helping those educating and preparing for practice in health and social work (through qualifying and post-qualifying courses) to appraise and use social research. It seeks through this to help create 'research mindedness' in practitioners. This fits very much with the concerns that practice be 'evidence based' or 'knowledge based'. In order to do this we need to look at the processes by which practitioners may incorporate findings into their work, as well as the nature of those findings. In relation to the latter, this requires them to understand something about how research is conducted, and how these reflect different approaches and beliefs about knowledge and the social world. In all these respects, the book aims to help develop informed practitioners who feel comfortable with using findings in the knowledge that they understand the nature and limitations of research.

This inevitably involves us looking, in a considerable proportion of the book, at methods. Because of its focus on this area, the book has a second use: that of introducing practitioners and educators, and those aspiring to practice (students), to some of the main methods by which they may themselves conduct research. This is also important for developing health and social services that take account of the perspectives of service users. The book, in other words, enables those who are qualifying, or who wish to consider the use of research in practice, to acquaint themselves with some of the most important dimensions of research.

While this book is intended to be introductory, it is hoped that it can also be used as a reference work by students, practitioners and educators to aid them in their understanding of research, and so lead them to contribute to better practice or to conduct research themselves. It will, it is hoped, make a contribution to both undergraduate and Masters courses in health and social work, and to the work (and research) of practitioners.

CHAPTER ONE

Introduction

Suppose you are a social services or health services manager. You are interested in developing services for minority ethnic groups in your area. How should you do this? Well, you might draw upon your experience, and that of others with whom you work, in an attempt to develop appropriate resources. Quite obviously you could look to the community itself, and get their advice. These two possible routes involve referring to the immediate work and local contexts. However, you might develop ideas that 'reinvent the wheel'. You might, indeed, find out along the way that what you are attempting has been tried before, and has not been successful. Or you may not know, one way or another, whether it ever *has* been successful.

How do you get round these problems? Well, you might draw on previous research. There may be findings from other areas that indicate the kinds of 'needs' of minority ethnic groups. There may be findings that describe attempts to respond to those needs, and the outcome of those attempts. This could be extremely useful. Such information could guide your developments, preventing you repeating the mistakes of others. It makes sense, therefore, that you should use those findings.

But it may not be that straightforward. Can we actually take findings at face value? We may be able to. But there are important issues that need to be confronted. What, for example, is the relevance of those findings to your circumstances? The research may have been carried out in the same kind of area, or one quite different in crucial respects. Demographic features may differ (one area may, for example, have a lower age profile than another). The social or economic circumstances may also differ – what, for example, of the difference between rural and urban areas, or between predominantly working-class or middle-class areas?

We can go beyond this. How was the research carried out? Were there a few interviews carried out with some service users, and were they detailed and qualitative? Was it a survey? If so, how were those who took part chosen? How do we know that the information gained from the research was representative of the area studied? Indeed, how do we know if the research could be generalized – that is applied widely to other areas?

I could go on. One point is that there is more than one source of guidance for the manager or practitioner in the human services. They can rely on their own professional experience. They can ask others for whom issues and developments are relevant. But they may also draw on research or knowledge that can provide crucial information relevant to our situation.

A second point, however, is that research may be extremely useful. It can help guide us in our actions, and make those actions more rational and well informed. It may, in principle, lead to more efficient and effective services. However, findings are almost never straightforward, and need themselves to be appraised in order to be able to use them properly. Questions like: How was the research conducted? How relevant is it to us? How far may findings be generalized? What was the quality of the research? are all important in considering how it may be used, and in which ways it can guide us. If you wish to use knowledge, then you need to be able to assess the nature and quality of that knowledge. Social and health professionals cannot just be in the business of applying knowledge. They need to be able to appraise that knowledge as well.

This example refers to resource development. But these points are no less relevant to the actions of individual practitioners, working with individual cases. Suppose you are working with a young man, in his early twenties, who is to be discharged from hospital. He has had a diagnosis of schizophrenia, but his illness has been stabilized. How do you make decisions about what to do?

Again, there may be much to be learned from practice. The experience of working for some time with people suffering from schizophrenia may have sensitized you to a range of issues that tend to recur time and again. You can talk to colleagues who also have experience. Consulting with the patient and his family is, of course, also important. However, where you do these things alone, you rely on your own experiences, and on those of people immediately around you; these experiences may be idiosyncratic. Patients and relatives also have their own experiences to call upon, but they cannot furnish you with information on matters about which they have no experience.

One way of informing yourself more broadly is to become aware of research into the discharge of patients from psychiatric hospital. In calling upon research you are going beyond the immediate experiences of you, your colleagues and the patient and his family. What are the kinds of issues confronted by patients diagnosed with schizophrenia when they are discharged from hospital? What are their implications for the patient and his family? What kinds of responses have been made, and with what degree of success?

These are legitimate lines of inquiry, and there is considerable information in the literature to help guide practitioners in this situation. However, the same kinds of questions arise as those confronted by our managers considering the issue of developing resources for minority ethnic groups. It is not just a matter of: What did the research say? It is also: How relevant is it for us? How was it carried out? What is the quality of the work? How reliable is it as a guide to what we wish to do?

Again we are faced with the issue, not simply of the application of findings, but of just how are you to appraise it? What is needed, in other words, is not just some slavish application of research, but a capacity to use good-quality research, and to know how it may best be applied. It is also the case that we need to recognize that different kinds of research may be useful for different elements of practice. For example, surveys may be useful to identify the characteristics or opinions of particular groups, such as minority ethnic groups. Examining change resulting from interventions may be achieved through some kind of social experimental design. Evaluating quality of services may be achieved through a service users' study.

It is clearly the case now that a wide range of research findings are available for those who work in the human services. Where these are capable of making practice better, more effective, more relevant to clients or service users, and so on, it is vital that practitioners are able to make use of the research. Research can transcend the idiosyncratic experiences and 'knowledge' of the individual practitioner. Where rigorously conducted, it has the advantage of being more general and more reliable than individual experience. It can also confront issues that may not have occurred to individual practitioners. We need, though, to know how to use it.

Evidence-based practice

The general importance of being able to use research in practice has been very much associated in recent years with the 'Evidence-Based Practice' movement.

'Evidence-based practice' has become the clarion call to the appropriate and efficient use of knowledge in practice. We hear it constantly, through government policy documents, publications and educational processes. The idea is, basically, that practitioners should use 'best evidence' to inform their practice, and to make judgements about the intervention that should take place. Health and social work professionals should be well-informed users of formal knowledge in the conduct of their practice.

What, however, is 'best evidence'? How do we choose between one form of evidence and another? Is it simply a matter of 'applying written knowledge'? Almost no one thinks that it is, yet there are few books seeking to confront this specific issue in health and social work literature. There are those who consider evidence-based practice to be unavoidably associated with the randomized controlled trial (RCT) that constitutes the 'gold standard' of research. RCTs are the classic form of experiment, a methodology applied in social research, as well as other areas, such as medicine. It is basically a comparative approach, in which changes in one group, receiving the experimental treatment, are compared with those in another, not receiving this treatment.

Others disagree profoundly, suggesting that ascribing such status to RCTs undermines the equally valuable contribution of other research. As a result, some use evidence-based practice in a broader way. Instead of seeing RCTs as its key manifestation, it is used to define an approach that uses all appropriate forms of knowledge for practice. This is a more eclectic approach to knowledge use, the kind of thing that the 'Making Research Count' movement, characterizing the relationship between a number of universities and local agencies, is noted for.

At the heart of this is a problem. How do we decide what consists of 'best evidence'? What are practitioners to do when they see a piece of research? How do they decide how valuable it is? This is not just a matter of application and applicability. It is about appraising the research itself. What is the quality of the research? Social scientists recognize that research can be of different qualities, so what is the quality of any piece or area of research that the professional may wish to use to guide practice? Social scientists also recognize that different methodologies, which characterize the range of social research, contain different assumptions that are rarely clearly stated in the research reports or findings themselves. These assumptions will be an important issue in the chapters to come.

Another issue is the methods themselves. If we are looking at a survey, how should it have been carried out? What should we be looking for when appraising a survey for its relevance to policy and practice? As practitioners, we need to know what a survey should entail, its different forms, and so on, in order to be able to appraise the research for use in practice. This requires an understanding of the methods of social research used in health and social work.

In short, we need to look beneath the surface of findings, and to understand the nature and quality of the research undertaken. If we are to take on board the idea of 'best evidence', we also need to be aware of 'garbage in, garbage out'. It's absolutely no good hoping to improve practice with poor research findings.

Developing guiding principles and understanding

How do we ensure that practitioners are able both to identify and use good, rather than poor, research findings, and are aware of the strengths and limitations of any particular research? This is not a straightforward question, yet it is one to which we can develop answers if a systematic approach is taken. Practitioners clearly need guidance in how to view and apply research to practice. *This book seeks to provide students, educators, practitioners and managers with the knowledge through which they can judge and use research which is relevant for their practice.* Such guidance would seek to examine two key issues:

- How can we appraise research that is relevant to practice?
- What are the key processes and issues in making use of such research in practice?

Perhaps surprisingly, there are no general books that systematically attempt to deal with, and link, *both* issues, despite their major importance for practitioners in an evidence-based environment. What we have is books that deal with one or other aspect of research appraisal or research use about which we are concerned. Generally, there are three types of books involved: those on developing capabilities in research; applied knowledge books, which nevertheless fail to engage with the *processes* involved; and specific knowledge form books.

'How to do research' books

There are, of course, myriad books that teach research methodology, rather than teaching how to examine the production of findings in relation to their use for practice. They are essentially about training people to do research. These are overwhelmingly sociological or psychological texts, and are of a 'how to do' variety ('How should you conduct a research project?'). There are occasional books of this sort for social work or nursing. Some are general (and very large and technical), such as Rubin and Babbie (2001), while others focus on specific aspects of research, such as qualitative (e.g. Padgett 1998; Shaw and Gould 2001) or feminist (e.g. Fawcett *et al.* 2000). They not about the use of research in practice.

'Applied knowledge' books

Some books seek to 'apply' knowledge to practice (e.g. Cormack 2000; Gillies 2002; Smith and Hunt 1997). These implicitly define the relation of knowledge to practice as 'applied knowledge' – here there is a piece of knowledge, and this is the practice to which it should be applied – and hence fail to engage with the *process of using that knowledge*. We now know a great deal more about the process of thinking through which research, and life experience, may be incorporated into the practice process. This element is a significant feature of the most recent research on knowledge, including pathfinding work conducted by the author (Sheppard 1995, 1998a; Sheppard and Ryan 2003; Sheppard *et al.* 2000, 2001).

'Specific knowledge form' books

Other books seek to apply knowledge, but focus on specific areas, such as attachment theory (e.g. Howe 1996) or social networks (e.g. Payne 1993), or on theories for practice, such as task-centred (e.g. Doel and Marsh 1992). Apart from the fact that they focus on a specific knowledge area, they tend to approach knowledge use as an issue of application, rather than as one of examining the implications of the process of knowledge development for practice use. They are, of course, confined to very specific areas. Where books seek to be more general, they can take the form of relevant knowledge forms for areas of practice, as with Tanner and Lindeman (1991), who focus on areas such as nursing care of children, adults, mental health, maternity, and so on. The result is a conglomeration of areas of knowledge that pays no attention to the implications of knowledge development for practice.

This book

To link the appraisal and application of research it is necessary to incorporate the most recent understanding of the processes of using knowledge in practice. This book attempts to do this in an easily accessible and readable way, in a manner which helps the reader to learn (adopting some principles from 'open learning'), while covering the areas of both health and social work.

The aims of the book are as follows:

1. to identify key issues in evidence-based practice, and the use of that evidence in practice

2. to examine the processes of knowledge use and application in health and social work

3. to identify the range of methodologies used in health and social work and related research, and to examine the manner through which rigorous research is defined within these methodologies

4. to examine the assumptions underlying the different methodologies, and subject them to critical appraisal, in a manner suitable for health and social work

5. to enable learners to follow the whole process of appraisal of evidence, from the assumptions underlying research to its actual use in practice.

This book will also be characterized by a number of themes that will make it more accessible to the reader, while remaining authoritative. Overall, these involve the use of techniques through which the reader may be able to consider and apply the lessons from this book. These include, in relation to each topic area:

- the examination of the ways in which research was conducted in areas relevant to social and health work, making specific reference to particular research

- the use of questions within the text by which the reader may begin to think how the methodologies themselves may inform the conduct of their practice

- the identification of key issues at the end of the chapter, in the form of exercises, through which the reader can explore their understanding of the contents of the chapter

- exercises involving exemplars of research, in the form of articles, which may be used, individually or in groups, to explore the appraisal and use of relevant research in practice.

Two further themes permeate the book. First, targeted references are used to provide readers with both exercises and further detailed reading. The targeting of referencing means the reader is not overwhelmed by a detailed bibliography; targeted references are deliberately limited, yet highly relevant. Second, examples from research, in health and social work, are used to enable the reader to consider how particular research approaches manifest themselves in findings that are relevant for practice. These include work by a range of authors in the field, and some of my own work. The advantage of using the latter is that it can give the reader a stronger 'feel' for the methodologies and their application, through a more direct contact with the author's own research.

The book will be largely (but not entirely) organized according to the key methodologies employed in research in social work and health. However, this is not done, as is the case with purely methodological texts, to explicate the methodologies for their own sake. It is done to allow practitioners, managers and educators to look beyond mere findings in health and social work, and to enable them to assess issues of relevance and quality in the process of considering and using research for practice. Our concern here is very much with identifying the implications of the use of such methods for practice.

After this introductory chapter, Chapter Two raises some key questions for the practitioner wishing to use social research for practice. It also focuses on the manner by which information, including that involving research, is brought to bear upon cases by practitioners, providing, so to speak, a 'psychological' or 'cognitive context' for our understanding of research appraisal and use.

Chapter Three takes this further by examining some key issues in the appraisal of social research. We discuss here how the nature of what constitutes knowledge is a matter of some disagreement, and this is a significant matter in considering when and how any form of knowledge may be used. We identify issues such as objects and subjects, voluntarism and causation, and the reasoning processes underlying different approaches to research. We then examine the ways in which a practical critical appraisal of research may be undertaken, one which does not rely on any particular methodology. We focus on issues such as problem formulation, literature review, findings and conclusions.

Chapters Four to Six focus on key elements of methodologies tending towards quantitative findings. Chapter Four examines the nature and development of structured questionnaires, including their conceptual and empirical underpinnings, and key issues of reliability and validity. These are not only important facets in the development of questionnaires, but also standards against which to measure research that develops and uses questionnaires that may be considered for practice.

Chapter Five deals with surveys and sampling. Again we examine facets of these approaches to help the reader to judge research for practice that has employed these methods. Issues of representativeness, sampling frame, forms of sampling and survey, as well as presentation of findings, are examined and appraised.

Chapter Six looks at experimental (and quasi-experimental) designs, approaches much loved by some in the evidence-based movement. They are particularly significant methodologies for those wishing to measure outcome, or to evaluate practice or programme performance. Issues of design, comparability, and internal and external validity are all examined again with the aim in mind of giving practitioners an appreciation of the ways in which such designs should be carried out, their limitations, and the issues of their use for practice.

Chapters Seven to Ten switch the focus to qualitative approaches to research. Chapter Seven looks at the qualitative interview. Practitioners may find similarities to the professional interview, and it can be instructive to compare the two. This looks at where it is appropriate, different forms of interview, and key elements in the conduct of the interview.

Chapter Eight looks at ethnographic methods. This is again interesting, since its emphasis on interviews, documents and, in particular, observation again makes it similar in many respects to the conduct of practice. This chapter may also benefit, from the reader's point of view, from a comparison with practice. The assumptions underlying ethnography are examined, key elements in the process of conducting ethnographic research are looked at, and a critical appraisal is conducted. As with other chapters, a focus is kept on its relevance, and use as a method, for findings informing practice.

Chapter Nine looks at content analysis and grounded theory. This concentrates, to a considerable degree (though not entirely), on processes of analysis. Issues such as grounding, meaning, development of themes and concepts are the subject matter for this chapter. The kinds of research produced using this method, and its use for practice, are considered at the end.

Chapter Ten is on the use of qualitative methods for evaluation. This looks at types of evaluation, research with and on service users, the significance of meaning for evaluation, and the relationship between process and outcome.

Chapter Eleven brings together qualitative and quantitative methods. While there are those who consider these two methods to be based on quite different approaches to knowledge development, others consider that the two approaches may complement each other. This chapter examines the ways in which the methods may be used together, and the particular contributions of each approach.

A short Afterword seeks to bring together the key themes to emerge from the previous chapters in a way that enables the reader to get an overview of the important issues when considering the use of research for practice.

A final initial comment may be made. The book is, as we have seen, designed to help social and health workers in the use of research knowledge for practice, by clarifying many of the key issues in the conduct of research. Of course, in the process, it is necessary for us to explain some of the key themes in research methodology. As a result, the book can serve the additional purpose of providing an introduction to the conduct of research itself, for those practitioners who wish to conduct such research. This is important, in so far as busy practitioners may have the time to carry this out. Research can provide a useful way of extending our knowledge and basing developments in local areas on firmer ground than would be the case if based simply on managerial whim, or local prejudice. It is to be hoped, therefore, that practitioners will find this a useful handbook, helping them identify key facets of the research process.

Having thus outlined the book as a whole, we shall now turn to the processes by which research use can become a feature of practice.

CHAPTER TWO

The Process of Using Social Research

Knowledge for practice

Much has been made in recent years about the importance of knowledge for practice in the health and social work professions. The latest term to be used, as we have mentioned, is 'evidence-based practice', the meaning of which can vary according to the person who is using it (Geyman, Deyo and Ramsey 2000). On the one hand, it can be used to denote any form of knowledge that might be deemed useful for practice. On the other hand, it can refer to a 'hierarchy of knowledge' – the belief amongst some that certain forms of 'knowledge', or in particular methods, provide more robust information and grounding for practice than other forms. Traditionally amongst such thinkers, it is the randomized controlled trial (of which much more later) that provides the gold standard for knowledge, and all knowledge generated by other methods has a lower status.

Of course, this generates questions about what exactly is knowledge. If one form of knowledge is better than another, does this mean that only the 'gold standard' knowledge constitutes 'real' knowledge? Does it mean that the rest is not knowledge at all, but something else? How about 'horses for courses'? Could it mean that some forms of knowledge are more useful in some circumstances than others?

Well, it could. We could be interested in the question: Are there ways of practising of which clients or service users approve more, and which engage them better, than others? That question may be best answered by asking people who are the subject of intervention. On the other hand, we might ask whether one form of intervention is more effective than another: Does a particular approach to child tantrums lead to a greater reduction (of the tantrums) than other approaches? We may be better off here looking at some kind of experiment, in which intervention A is compared over a period of time with intervention B, to discover whether it does indeed lead to a greater reduction in frequency of tantrums.

Whatever your position on these matters, what this suggests is that there is a range of approaches underlying the findings that constitute social research, findings that we may be urged to use to provide a more responsive, effective or rational response to client or service user needs. These approaches are generally called methods, or methodologies, in social research. They are the ways in which researchers go about collecting and analysing the data that provide the basis for knowledge or evidence-based practice.

Beyond this, however, is the question: How far do we have information that is relevant and useful for practice? Well, we know there is an awful lot of social research. Much of it lies outside the remit or concerns of particular professionals. The social rituals of South Sea islanders may, for example, qualify as information that is not necessarily very helpful for those in the health or social work professions in Europe or the United States. Even, however, in the realm of health and social work, there are large gaps in our knowledge – we simply do not know what is going on, or what is most effective in relation to some problems. What do we do then? Do we rely on our own personal experience? Or on the accretion of practice wisdom over time?

Well, yes. There can be little doubt that there are limits to social research, in particular its applicability to practice. Some of this is due to the absence of research in some areas. Other reasons include the ways in which social research is conducted. Much of it is designed to collect general information. Even, for example, where research indicates that more women suffering depression find it difficult to engage in partnership with professionals than those without depression, this does not mean that this particular woman – the one you are seeing as part of your intervention – will be more difficult to engage in partnership because she is depressed.

One issue then is that social research operates at the level of the general, while each case mostly involves the practitioner operating at the level of the individual, or particular circumstance. How far are we able to apply general findings to the particular situation of the person or case that we have in front of us? When we confront – as a health visitor, social worker, teacher or general medical practitioner – a case of possible child abuse, how are we to use the research knowledge we have on child abuse, to help us in our practice?

Another issue is the probabilistic nature of findings. Even the most carefully conducted studies, which seek to be most representative, will not provide findings that apply to every instance – that is to every particular case. Many depressed women may have problematic partnerships with professionals, but not all depressed women. Furthermore, there is often more than one factor influencing any particular set of actions or behaviour. The personality of the practitioner, as well as the depression, may well affect the situation. Some practitioners may be better than others at creating partnerships in these circumstances. Whether or not the woman has the morale support of a partner may also affect things.

The point is that in social life we cannot build in every factor that influences every situation we are seeking to understand. The best, most generalizable, research will fall short of providing 100 per cent coverage of all situations. We are then looking at information that can help provide *guidance*, and *better-informed judgements*, but not certainty. We may almost universally be sure that tonsillitis will improve with the impact of antibiotics (but even this is not wholly universal), but we cannot be sure that cognitive behavioural therapy will lead to a reduction in depression in any particular case.

Indeed, we are here talking of research that purports to provide information that may be generalized – that might apply (probabilistically) to any particular situation. However, some research does not even purport to generalize. Some single-case studies carried out by ethnographers (again, more of which later) are only intended to provide information on that particular case study. We cannot really tell, and the researchers would not claim that we could tell, how far that information is applicable to all situations. Because we look at interactions in one particular home for the elderly does not mean that we can generalize from this to all homes for the elderly.

This is a problem which has further implications for health and social work professions. Many studies are carried out opportunistically – often because researchers are provided with somewhere to carry out the research and it is relatively convenient. This can extend to approaches that use measures usually designed to allow the researcher to generalize – for example, sampling and carrying out surveys. We may have information on child health practice in one particular authority, but we cannot be sure that this practice extends to other authorities. How well, therefore, are the findings suited to our practice? How far can we usefully apply them to situations that may not always be those outlined in the research?

This all sounds very pessimistic, but there is really much that is positive. There may be limitations to all research – indeed there are – but that does not mean that it cannot prove useful. One clear example, relevant for both health and social work professions, is the research on expressed emotion and schizophrenia. There is now ample evidence that high levels of expressed emotion (particularly critical comments) by relatives of someone suffering from schizophrenia create a significantly higher rate of relapse. This is clearly useful. We need to employ methods that will reduce the likelihood of relapse in such families. This can be achieved either by reducing the level of expressed emotion, or by reducing the amount of contact with the high-expressed-emotion relatives. This straightforward example (based on well-conducted research) shows that research can be useful to practitioners, and that it is important to make use of it when we have it.

Social research can be highly useful to the practitioner. However, it is general and probabilistic, and there are different types that may be useful in different ways. Hence its use needs to become a significant part of the practitioner's judgement, and incorporated in his or her 'thinking processes'.

Approaches to social research: Their importance for the practitioner

We have already mentioned, in our discussion on evidence-based practice, that there are different types of research. If we are to use research, we need to ask: What kind of research is it that we are dealing with? This is highly important. This also involves the question: What is the nature and validity of the particular research you are using in practice? In short, how are you to judge the usefulness of research for practice? This involves two initial issues:

1. What kinds of assumptions or approaches to the social world are made in a particular piece of social research?

2. How well has that research been carried out, in the light of rigorous research practice?

These questions then link into, and indeed inform, a third:

3. How useful is a particular piece of research for practice, and how may it be applied?

The answers to these questions can help the practitioner judge the quality of the research, which helps them in turn to determine its relevance and usefulness to practice. The informed practitioner, in other words, does not simply know what the research says, but also is able to judge the quality and relevance of that research.

It is to these issues that this book is devoted. In order to judge research, we need to understand the range of research on offer, its strengths and weaknesses, and then to be able to consider how it may be used in practice. This is a long road, but it requires us to:

- understand the range of social research methods employed in relation to health and social work

- be aware of the assumptions adopted through the employment of the research

- consider how the findings that may be related to practice were generated, and the strengths and weaknesses of the findings

- consider, in the light of the above, the relevance and applicability of those findings to practice – indeed, how they may be applied.

This is how we intend to proceed with this book.

Using research means appraising it. This in turn means that the practitioner needs to be aware that there are different approaches, or methodologies, and that these may be more or less suitable for different kinds of practice issues. The practitioner needs also to know that research can be of variable quality, and hence to be able to judge that quality. They further need to be able to critically appraise these approaches.

Incorporating research into practice

It is also important, however, not to start our thinking at the level of knowledge, but at the 'case level'. We need to start with the situation to which knowledge needs to be applied. Why is this? Well it is simple. That is how the practitioner sees things. Research is useful, and useable, only when applied through the 'eyes' of the practitioner. The key here is that the practitioner confronts a particular situation. They need to be sufficiently aware, and knowledgeable, to be able to use the evidence in relation to the particular work they are undertaking. It is perhaps instructive to consider how this happens.

There is a great deal of research on expertise and decision making. Considerable interest has been shown on the matter of reasoning and clinical decision making in both health and social work (e.g. Dowie and Elstein 1988; Higgs and Jones 1995; Thompson and Dowding 2002). However, it is in social work that the step-by-step incorporation of knowledge alongside experience has perhaps been examined most closely (Sheppard and Ryan 2003; Sheppard *et al.* 2000, 2001).

The central question is: How do practitioners think about situations with which they are confronted, and how do they incorporate formal knowledge (or research, if you will) into their practice? The evidence from social work is that there are three major dimensions:

- a process of critical appraisal, which occurs from the beginning of referral
- a process of hypothesis generation and testing
- the generation of implicit rules, through which general knowledge or experience is conveyed to the specific practice situation.

This all lies in the area of cognition, or thinking and reasoning. In psychology, and some of the health professions, this has been considered in the literature on reasoning and decision making, as to some extent has the notion of the reflective practitioner (Schön 1987, 1991). In social work, it has been specifically developed into the notion of 'process knowledge' (from earlier notions of, first, reflection, and next reflexivity).

What kinds of things are we talking of here? Well basically, as any practitioner knows, there is no straightforward process of application of knowledge to practice. At a minimum the practitioner needs to be able to identify salient characteristics of a situation, through which they can then begin to consider what to do about it. If they are to consider the application of research knowledge to practice, then they need to be able to identify relevant areas of knowledge and research. If you are looking at how well a young mother is managing with her children you may wish to call upon literatures on parenting, developmental psychology and coping. If you are interested in the reaction of a newly admitted patient to hospital you may wish to call upon literature on the 'sick role'. If you want to know how a woman will respond to being told that she will require a mastectomy, you may be interested in literature on loss or anticipatory grief.

This much is about synchronizing knowledge areas with those of the situation about which you are concerned. Of course formal (written and researched) knowledge is not the only source of guidance to practitioners. They may draw on experience gained from practice or from their life in general. This can be necessary in areas for which we have no research findings, or the findings are too general for use in the specific instance. The experienced practitioner is liable, therefore, to draw upon those three areas – formal knowledge, specifically social research, practice experience, and life experience – to provide them with guidance in relation to any particular practice issue or problem.

Social research is useful for particular reasons. First, social research methodologies should (if used properly) bring to bear on a problem greater rigour in the collection and analysis of information than would be expected by an individual just drawing upon their own experience. Second, social research does not in general draw upon individual instances, but on the analysis of a number of cases, from which we are able to draw wider inferences. Third, the research represents the accumulation of information from those who have made it their purpose (collectively) to study particular areas of social life. They are, collectively, the repository of considerable and developed expertise. Fourth, much of the research seeks to be generalizable; that is, relevant, and applicable, to similar situations. Hence, social research is able to lift us above the limits of our personal experience, and that of those immediately around us, and above the potential 'tyranny of the anecdote'.

Whatever the source of guidance, however, the actual processes of using these sources are broadly similar. I shall refer here to the potential range of processes of thinking about a case available to the practitioner.

Collectively, practitioners have demonstrated these modes of thinking in their practice. However, that doesn't mean that all practitioners actually use all these processes. To the extent they do not, however, it becomes more difficult for them to integrate social research into their practice and, arguably, reduces the quality and rigour of their practice.

Critical appraisal

Critical appraisal refers to analysis undertaken by practitioners through which, at the referral stage, they seek to make initial judgements about the nature and quality of the information they have received. Referrals are not straightforward pieces of information, but require such appraisal. The process of critical appraisal, however, although vital at the outset, remains crucial throughout, if practitioners are to remain 'alive' to possible developments and changes.

There are various elements to critical appraisal. These include:

- focused attention
- querying and evaluating information
- making causal inferences.

FOCUSED ATTENTION

Focused attention refers to the particular facets of a case that the practitioner considers the most salient. In any particular case, there are potentially many (perhaps infinitely many) facets upon which the practitioner could focus. However, in order to make sense, and to respond in a considered way, they focus on particular facets. For example, where there is a concern about child abuse, they will want to concentrate on particular aspects of the alleged abuse, perhaps aspects of the child or the parent, and maybe related events contemporary to the alleged abuse. These by no means provide all potential areas, but without such focus, the practitioner can make no sense.

Focused attention is important for its potential link with research. For example, in a case of alleged child abuse, one area that the practitioner may wish to look at closely is the parents' own background. What were their own experiences of being parented? What was their relationship with their own parents? What did they 'learn' about parenting behaviour? Focused attention allows us to link with formal knowledge. Where we are interested in such questions, information on the nature and explanations for 'intergenerational transmission' of abuse becomes relevant. Here we have the process by which the particular practice problem is synchronized with the research literature.

QUERYING AND EVALUATING INFORMATION

Querying and evaluating information are, likewise, relevant to referrals, but also to the processes of communication and information exchange during intervention generally. At the heart of this is a refusal to accept information purely at face value. Where comments or allegations are made, the practitioner needs to be able to investigate, critically, whether they are true. Where a mental health assessment is being made, statements may be made by individuals relating to the patient's behaviour. They may allege they are difficult or behaving in strange ways. Is this just that individual's perspective on the situation? Or do others share it? What exactly is the form of behaviour that they regard to be strange? And how does it differ from their behaviour at other times?

We may wish to evaluate risk in this process, and we are again relating our thinking in relation to the case, to the potential use of social research (Sheppard 1990). What are the processes by which we should think about risk? And what do we know about risk factors in this situation? How, therefore, should we regard this situation? This is particularly the case where others are alleging that the situation is fraught with risk. How far is this confirmed (or falsified) by our use of risk analysis?

MAKING CAUSAL INFERENCES

A further element of critical appraisal is 'causal inferences'. This refers to inferences made by practitioners from information they initially receive, which could then be built into hypotheses about underlying features about the problem or situation. It is about 'going behind' statements made in the initial information received, in an attempt to make more sense of the situation. If we find that there are concerns about the parenting by a grandparent of an early teenage grandson (where both parents have died), we may begin to think what may be behind this. Is it an unresolved grief reaction? Has the young person never confronted or dealt with the grief they felt over the loss of their parents? Is this affecting the way they are relating to their grandparents (who have parental responsibility)? Alternatively, is this a matter of a 'generation gap'? Do the problems arise from different expectations of what a young teenager should be allowed to do? Maybe this is about 'being a teenager'. Perhaps they are simply going through a 'difficult period'.

These causal inferences are most clearly identifiable at the early stages of an intervention (before the practitioner has got to know the situation well), and where they are, in effect, developing hypotheses of why events seem to be happening as they do. However, case management generally involves the accretion of information, and the new information will need to be re-evaluated, which again may involve causal inferences. These inferences help indicate the direction of an assessment and, further along, the intervention.

Critical appraisal is a major element of the practitioner's conduct of their practice. It is particularly important at the outset but, in rigorous practice, continues throughout the lifetime of the case, as the practitioner subjects his or her and others' perceptions to constructive appraisal. It is also one of the processes by which research may be incorporated into practice.

Hypothesis generation and testing: The interrelationship between hypotheses and evidence in practice

We are going to hear a great deal more about hypotheses later in the book, and I don't want to consider them in too much detail at this stage. However, hypotheses or provisional hypotheses, form an important element of the practitioner's thinking processes. When practitioners think about a case they seek to form some particular idea about it. They need to answer the questions: What is the problem? How can that problem be explained? And how should I deal with it? Now, in relation to any particular situation with which the practitioner is confronted, there is always more than one possible way to look at it.

At its simplest, consider the position of the general medical practitioner. They see a patient, and rely on the patient to describe aspects of their health. What are they to make of it? The patient will identify various facets of their health functioning, and these will provide clues as to what is wrong. From these descriptions, the GP may form hunches of the kind of problem they are confronting. If they receive information on a sore throat, and pain in the ear, together with a runny nose, they may think it is a virus (generally), just a cold-related problem, tonsillitis or something else. Each of these possibilities represents a provisional hypothesis. By asking further questions, the GP may be able to 'firm up' their diagnosis. On that basis (say they consider it tonsillitis), they will seek some kind of remedy, perhaps penicillin. This may work, but what if the patient begins to feel nauseous? They may then consider that this is some kind of allergic reaction, and use an alternative antibiotic. It is hoped this will then work, and the illness will be resolved. However, identifying each problem at each stage – the illness, the allergic reaction, and the solution – involves making hypotheses. They may be right or wrong, and we will only be able to tell by the accumulating information that arises because of the diagnosis and responses.

This is, of course, an example based on biological rather than social research knowledge. The principles of 'process thinking' are, however, the same. The social worker who is faced with a possible child abuse referral, where the child has received a head injury, is faced with a similar process. What precisely are the injuries? How were they caused? Is this a case of child abuse, or is it something else? What, if anything, do we need to do about it? And what is most likely to be successful?

The answers to all these questions represent hypotheses, or provisional hypotheses. When we are trying to piece together what had happened, the injuries may have been accidental or non-accidental. Suppose they 'fell off a chair' and banged their head against a hard table (according to the parents). Is this plausible? Is it consistent with their injuries? If it is, how do we know they were not pushed? What is the other evidence we need to bring together in order to get to the most plausible understanding of what happened?

There are various conclusions we can come to: that the injuries were not consistent with the alleged causes; that they are consistent, and the explanation is plausible; that they are consistent and the explanation is implausible, but that it may well have been accidental nonetheless; or that it was probably non-accidental. In making these judgements other information will play a part: the practitioner would need to make some judgements about the parents. Suppose the practitioner concluded that the injury was not accidental. Well then they must begin to make sense of it. Why should the parents claim it was an accident? Is it because they were trying to 'cover up' a generally aggressive attitude, and set of behaviours, towards the child? Or could it be that, confronted with people in authority, they had panicked and made up the story?

We could go on, but I hope the reader has got the general idea. Each of these positions represents hypotheses, right to the end. Thus one hypothesis for our final example would be that this was one manifestation of generally aggressive behaviour towards the child (which had not, perhaps, yet come to light). Another would be that they had panicked, and were covering up for an exceptional event, which did not reflect their general level of parenting because they feared they might 'lose the child' (into care).

This is the kind of situation that can confront the whole team of practitioners involved with child abuse, whether health or social work. Health visitors, accident and emergency staff, paediatricians, GPs and of course social workers deal routinely with situations not far removed from the one described. They have very difficult decisions to make, many that the majority of the population would find a tremendous burden.

We have found that practitioners make hypotheses about the whole case (this is a case of child abuse, or this is not a case of child abuse), and aspects of it (this was done in a fit of temper, or it was done while mucking about; the explanation was the result of fear of authority figures, and so on). Those which cover the whole case we have termed 'whole-case hypotheses', and those which cover only one aspect of the case we have called 'partial-case hypotheses'. The practitioner, in analysing and progressing in the case, will move between hypothesis and evidence collection, each informing the other, in order to come to a point where they have reached some kind of 'definition of the situation'. The same will occur with interventions: they will attempt interventions and, as long as they are not complacent, will monitor the effect of the intervention for its outcome. The implicit hypothesis of any particular intervention is that it will achieve some objective (improving parenting through parenting classes, for example), but that may have to be revised in the light of the evidence.

Practitioners are unavoidably employing hypotheses in the conduct of their practice. The progressive use of these hypotheses, together with the preparedness to look at alternatives, forms the kernel of good practice.

The content of hypotheses and practice: Implicit rules

We now have some idea about the processes of thinking that emerge in the conduct of practice. We know that hypotheses are being continually generated to help make sense of, and respond to, a situation. But what about the content of these hypotheses? How do we decide what the hypothesis actually is?

This is very important, because it is in the generation of hypotheses that we are able to bring social research findings (or life or professional experience) to bear on a particular practice situation. How, in other words, we can bring the generality of social research findings to bear on the specifics of the practice situation confronted.

It is apparent that practitioners have a vast array of 'background rules' available for them to apply to a practice situation. They do not necessarily consciously think of them as rules, but they bring them to bear when confronting the range of situations characteristic of their work. The rules, which are descriptive, represent background 'knowledge' about the ways in which social situations work.

What does this mean in real terms? Well, the kind of rule we are talking about might be 'behavioural problems in children are [or can be] the result of inadequate bonding with an [adult] attachment figure'. Now this is not the only kind of rule that can operate. Another might be 'teenagers tend to be more difficult and behavioural problems can be the result of their life stage'. Both these rules relate to behavioural problems, but they are not necessarily consistent with each other. Indeed, they can be different or contradictory. This does not matter, because the practitioner is calling upon a range of alternative background rules that may be applied to a situation where there are child behaviour problems. The key is the 'adequacy of fit' between the rule being used and the situation confronted. Taking the two rules we have mentioned, it would be a matter of sorting out which of the two was most consistent with the client's circumstances.

These rules provide the bridge between social research findings and the immediate situations confronted, case by case, by the practitioner. Thus, we might be dealing with a young person with serious behavioural problems. In considering the possibility that this arose from inadequate bonding ('behavioural problems in children are [or can be] the result of inadequate bonding with an [adult] attachment figure') we are bringing together elements of attachment theory with the particular case with which the practitioner is dealing. In effect, where social research is used, it has been transformed into background rules that are available to be considered when appropriate (and sometimes clearly matching) circumstances are confronted.

This is not the only background rule that might be applied to the situation. Where (for example) a teenage girl is presenting challenging behaviour, there may be a range of possibilities. It may be because of inadequate bonding. It may, alternatively, be (hypothesized) that it is a 'phase' – that teenagers tend to act out, and it is part of personal development. There might also be considered to be some 'generation gap' in expectations, between parent and child, going on. A further explanation might be that there has been some form of sexual abuse, or that the young woman is being bullied at school. These, as we have suggested, do not have to agree. Indeed, these provide alternative possibilities, and it is through the interplay of investigation, evidence, rules and hypotheses that the practitioner moves towards achieving the most satisfactory definition of the situation (ideally, the one least likely to be wrong).

Now, clearly not all these rules, even those we have just mentioned, come from social research, or social science in general. For example, the idea that there might be a generation gap behind intergenerational conflict or that teenage behavioural problems are a 'phase they go through' are ideas widely held in society. That they are widely held (and therefore cannot really be called 'professional knowledge') does not invalidate them as potential hypotheses to explain a situation.

However, as we have suggested earlier, where conducted well, social research should have greater weight attached to it, as a guide to situations. For example, without an understanding of attachment theory or the consequences of sexual abuse, we may rather too easily conclude that teenage behavioural problems are the result, in a particular instance, of a 'phase' the young person is going through.

There is clearly, then, an important place for professional knowledge based on social research. Where it does emerge, it does so in the context of rules. For example a social worker may be aware that some sex offenders are interested in both sexes rather than confining themselves to one. When used to understand a situation where sex abuse may have occurred, they would have a rule such as 'sex offenders do not have an exclusive preference on the basis of sex in their choice of victims'.

Another issue may be about the cycle of abuse. Here practitioners may consider abuse is more likely where the perpetrator was abused as a child. The rule here would be 'someone who is abused in childhood may go on as an adult to abuse children him- or herself'.

Another area in which formal knowledge may play a part is in the use of 'technical language'. In social work the main source of technical language is concepts from the social sciences. These concepts are important because they 'give form' to what would otherwise be vaguely understood ideas about the way the social world operates. A term like 'expressed emotion' when used in relation to schizophrenia provides a way of looking at this mental health problem that would not be available without awareness of this issue. In the case of expressed emotion, research on intervention provides us with guidance as to effective practice. Concepts provide a basis on which to give meaning to – to make sense of – particular situations.

The content of the hypotheses used by practitioners, both to help them make sense of a situation and intervene, is determined through the use of rules, which practitioners are unlikely to think of as rules, although they will constantly use their content. The content of these rules can be derived from research, as part of formal knowledge, and provide the means through which practitioners may incorporate research into their practice.

We have now been able to demonstrate both the importance of social research, and how it can be used in practice. We can see, first of all, that the social research with which we should be concerned is 'practice relevant' – that is focused on issues directly relevant to practice. Nevertheless, social research is crucial in broadening and deepening professional horizons, and providing knowledge and evidence that can make considerable difference to the quality of practice. We know that in much of health and social work practice, it needs to be used alongside practice and life experience. Nevertheless, it provides a potentially crucial contribution to the practice process.

We have considered its importance and application. However, as we have already suggested, 'social research' is not a single entity, a set of information that may be applied directly to practice. Social research may be conducted well or badly, it may contain different kinds of data, it may be more or less widely applicable, it may be more or less limited, and it possesses assumptions about the social world that need to be considered. Using social research – no longer a matter of choice – requires us to understand its nature and validity.

CHAPTER THREE

Some Key Issues in Appraising Social Research

One of the key features marking out a profession is its use of knowledge. When, for example, we focus on the oldest professions, such as medicine and law, we find a strong knowledge base influencing their work, or so it seems. Thus, for medicine we find, generally, that the realm of the bio-physical – anatomy, physiology, and so on – informs their practice. In law, it is the detailed knowledge of the rules and regulations that make up the law, and the way they may be used in practice, which is most significant as a knowledge base. Alongside this goes fairly extensive periods of training. The basic length of training for a doctor is five years. This is then followed by further clinical training until they are able to become a member of one of the Royal Colleges. A long old haul!

Why is it that these professions place such importance on knowledge? It's fairly simple really: without that knowledge they could not carry out their day-to-day tasks. Imagine a judge who knew very little of the law – he or she would hardly be able to pronounce on the legality or otherwise of the processes of the conduct of a case, or be able to sit in expert judgement on the case itself. Better still, imagine a surgeon with no medical training (and to go alongside this a blunt knife!). Who, I wonder, would be prepared to entrust themselves to such a person. Certainly not me. In order to perform complex, life-threatening operations, a very high level of education and training is required. Indeed, the knowledge required for the job, and its enactment in practice, in many ways defines the nature of the job itself. A surgeon is not just someone who cuts people up. He is someone who is trained to do so in an informed manner, maximizing (we all dearly hope) the chance of a successful outcome to the surgery.

Evidence-based practice

So, where does knowledge reside in relation to human services professionals? And, indeed, what kind of knowledge might such professionals claim to be important? Well, many in social work and nursing have for some time sought to claim that their occupation is a profession, by dint of its use of knowledge. Some writers have sought to identify the key defining characteristics of a profession (generally by looking at doctors and lawyers) and see how closely they defined social work, nursing or teaching. Usually there is a gentle sigh of disappointment, and a statement that, while social work or nursing cannot qualify for the hallowed halls of the true professions, they can proclaim themselves semi-professions (whatever that is).

One of the problems is that some of the knowledge base of human services professionals appears so routine. Take social work. If I am a child and family social worker, what do I know that a mother with three or four children in their teens does not? What about if I don't have any kids myself? Some would say that I hardly qualify as very knowledgeable, and that there is no substitute for experience. If I am trying to help a mother with children whose behavioural problems are such that she is finding it difficult to cope, then maybe I would have more to offer if I had children, and had to confront the problems of bringing them up. This is certainly brought up time and again by some clients, and even by those not involved directly with social workers. 'How many children have you got?' they might say. Or 'You look a bit young to be a social worker'. Very undermining!

Such people will not have been alone. For many years the basic social work qualification in Britain has been below degree level, and taken less than three years (rather less than doctors). There was some resistance to giving social workers longer training, despite the child abuse deaths so widely reported in the media. The implication would be, however good or bad you may be as social workers, there is little point in extra training because it will make little difference in practice. One Minister of Health (Virginia Bottomley) suggested that what was really needed was 'streetwise grannies' (whatever they are).

Much the same could be said of health visitors, a profession whose concern, like many social workers, is with child and family care. The significance of 'life experience' is indeed one that is stressed across health and social work professions generally.

Things have changed considerably in recent years. There has been a far greater emphasis on learning as a basis for practice – hence, for example, the basic social work qualification is three years long, and to become fully qualified as a child care practitioner, it is expected that you take the child care award – a further year of education and training. Four years' training – more like the traditional professions now. These developments have been reflected in other professionals, with nursing and other health professionals entering universities for their basic qualifications.

Alongside this, something called 'evidence-based practice' has emerged in recent years. Evidence-based practice is something prized across health and welfare areas, such as nursing and medicine, as well as social work. The basic idea, with which few would disagree, is that practice informed by evidence is likely to be better practice. This is because we are able, through use of evidence, to draw upon knowledge of general relevance, and apply it to the individual situation.

However, there is a particular view of evidence-based practice that argues that there is a hierarchy of knowledge, with one form better than all the others. These people argue that randomized controlled trials [RCTs] provide the blue chip evidence for judging interventions, and that other possible methods are simply not as good and should not, therefore, be given as great an importance. This raises the intriguing questions: How is it that there are different 'kinds' of knowledge? And what is it that makes one type of knowledge more important than another?

Well, perhaps the rather startling truth is that there are indeed different types or forms of knowledge. What is more, some are widely seen to be good for doing some kinds of research, while others are seen as better for carrying out other research. However, we can go further than this. There is even some dispute about what is 'best knowledge', and even what we can know in the first place. Not everyone claims the RCT is the blue chip form of knowledge, some suggest that alternative forms of knowledge are more valid.

Some of this has a philosophical basis. While we will look at this to some extent, our main thrust will be at looking at the different approaches to carrying out research. What is the range of research conventionally used in health and social work? Where are they best applied? Are some forms of knowledge better than others? What strengths and weakness do they have? How can we decide what is the strongest form of knowledge generally, and what we should look to in particular research studies?

All this and more will be examined in relation to applied social research (which is the primary foundation for social work knowledge, and a major component of health professionals' knowledge). In the process you will, I hope, get a clearer idea about the ways research is carried out, its degree of validity, and its applicability to practice. However, before we can go to some of the details of particular methods, it is worth looking at some of the approaches to knowledge that underlie these different methods. This involves looking at issues of ontology (what exists) and epistemology (what we can know). It is to this that we shall first turn.

Do we have a formula for sorting this out? Some criteria by which we will 'know' what is the best approach to knowledge accretion? Social research for health and social work is underpinned by a notion of what constitutes knowledge. While many are eclectic about this (they are unworried if these underpinnings differ from each other), others are not. It is important to identify some basic facets of these differences.

Objects and subjects

There are two diverging positions about what we can know about the social world. One approach argues that there is a real and objective nature to things. There is a real outside world (including the social world) and our task as social scientists is to apprehend it. Reality is external to the individual, imposing itself on individual consciousness from outside the individual himself. The other sees 'reality' not as objective, but as subjectively generated by us as human beings. The human mind imposes its order on the world as it is perceived, and gives it meaning. It is a construct of the individual, or more broadly a 'social construct' of the society in which we live. What on earth does all this mean?

Objectivism

The objectivist sees the world as external to the individual. It is real, not just existing in the eye of the beholder. Reality, the objectivist thinks, exists independently from the individual's apprehension of it. It exists prior to the individual's personal existence. Furthermore, it has a direct bearing on the individual's development and circumstances, on their experiences and behaviour. Thus, we may talk of economic or social structures creating material conditions, but also having an impact on a person's outlook, understanding and awareness of their social world.

One of the most famous objectivists was Emile Durkheim (1952). He investigated the occurrence of suicide. He sought to demonstrate that it was the result of certain 'social facts', combining to produce particular acts of suicide. As different societies contain different types of social facts, we should expect suicide rates to vary between different cultures. The problem here was: What kind of social facts produce suicide (itself a social fact)?

Durkheim analysed official statistics on suicide in different European countries. On the basis of this he developed the ideas that the degree of social integration characterizing particular societies determined its number of suicides. Social integration was defined in terms of the number and closeness of relationships an individual has with others. There was an inverse relationship. This, of course, has considerable intuitive appeal. Hence:

- the greater the degree of social integration, the lower would be the rate of suicides
- the less the degree of social integration, the higher would be the rate of suicides.

The less involved an individual is with others, the more likely they would be to commit suicide. He found suicide was:

- more prevalent in Protestant countries than Catholic
- more prevalent in urban societies than rural
- more prevalent amongst the unmarried than married.

Higher levels of social integration, Durkheim thought, was evident in Catholic, rural and married situations than, respectively, Protestant, urban and unmarried situations. So, killing oneself seems to be a highly individual act. However, we can identify the objective social fact of social integration having a major impact on another objective social fact, committing suicide.

Subjectivism

For the subjectivist, the apparently objective, ordered nature of the social world is, in fact, the product of people's minds. There is no objective reality out there waiting to be discovered. People construct and impose patterns and relationships on social situations, through which they make sense of the situation. Meaning and interpretation of the social world is imposed by people themselves rather than being an apprehension of an objective reality external to themselves.

How the world is, or appears to be, can only be understood from the point of view of people directly involved in whatever activity is being considered. We can only understand parenting from the point of view of those involved, we can only understand social work or nursing actions through an understanding of the purpose and motivation of those involved. We have to 'occupy' the frame of reference of the participants in action – how they see the world.

Meaning – how we understand things – arises in the process of social interaction. How we understand our world and our relations with each other emerges through our interaction, and our interpretations of this. Humans, so to speak, 'make meaning'. There are, therefore, no social facts, only generated meanings. These are our interpretations, as individuals, or when such interpretations or meanings are shared, as cultural meanings.

What does the subjectivist make of suicide? Atkinson (1978) argues that social events take on meaning according to what those involved make of them. Suicide is simply something defined by certain people in relation to some deaths, but not others: defined by particular actors in the situation. One is looking to key figures, such as the coroner, the family, the doctor, and so on.

Atkinson did not assume that there is an objective act of suicide. Instead, he sought to ask: How are deaths categorized as suicide? What are the characteristics of the situation that encourage or discourage people to see someone's death as an act of suicide? Once we look at things this way, calling a death a suicide becomes more tricky. Some individuals will deliberately disguise their suicide to look like an accident. How many car deaths on lonely roads are in fact attempts to end their lives? Suicide carries a stigma, so families may prefer verdicts of accidental death.

This may help explain Durkheim's figures. Suicide may be a sinful, and damned, act for a Catholic, it does not receive the same censure from Protestants. Classifying a death as suicide in a Catholic country is not just an official statistic, it also dooms the individual to damnation.

Atkinson found that if the deceased possessed certain characteristics, their death was more likely to be seen as suicide in the courts. These were:

- drug overdose
- previous threat of suicide
- history of mental disturbance.

None of this is to deny that some people deliberately take their lives. What is at issue is which people, why, and who says they did.

For the subjectivist, such events, and what they mean to actors and observers, can only be understood at the level of individual subjectivities.

For the objectivist the world (including the social world) is external to the individual, who in principle can apprehend it clearly. For the subjectivist there is no objective reality out there waiting to be discovered. People construct and impose patterns and relationships on social situations, through which they make sense of the situation.

Voluntarism and causation

How do we generally seek to explain why people do things? This is an issue of central importance to the social scientist, and involves looking at voluntarism and causation.

Voluntarism

Voluntarism is the idea that we undertake actions of our own accord, and that we are therefore responsible for those actions and their consequences. We undertake actions because we choose to do so. It is our decision.

This is very much the way in which we view our everyday lives. If we decide to cross the road, it is because we want to cross the road. Maybe it's a hot day and there's an ice cream van on the other side. We choose to cross the road in order to get an ice cream, which will refresh us and make us feel less hot. Likewise, I come to a lecture because I choose so to do. No one is forcing me, but it's just so interesting that I would really like to be there. So I am.

We can't be surprised at this reasoning, because it is, to a considerable degree, an expression of our 'taken for granted' thoughts in our everyday lives. How, for example, can we like or dislike someone, or judge them to be good or bad, unless we think they are acting of their own free will? Where someone does me a favour, or goes out of their way to help me out in a difficult situation, we are able to think well about them because we think they decided themselves to do it. It was not some automatic or autonomic response, but a decision that they made voluntarily.

We look at actions in terms of the intentions and motivations of those concerned. Why should someone choose to go to university? It could be because they want to develop their education. It might be because they want to have better career prospects, or that they want to earn more money. The expression of their choice is understandable in terms of their intentions and motivation.

The same goes for the actions of a parent. Why did they just hit their five-year-old hard? It could be because they felt the child was being deliberately naughty in taking some biscuits having been told not to do so. This was not the first time they had done this. They had been warned. Reasoning with them had not worked. They might also feel that slapping a child is not only right and proper in the appropriate situations, but also that it is an effective way of achieving their ends (a better-behaved child).

We need not labour this issue. It is so embedded in the way we view the world that it should appear quite familiar. It is even at the heart of our judicial system.

Causation

People's actions may not be ascribed by the social scientist to their own voluntary choice. There is an alternative way of viewing things: they may be the product of forces and factors in the world that you cannot control and may not even recognize. Your actions, in short, may be caused by something.

To simplify matters, let's first look at the physical world. What about apples – specifically Newton's apple? Why did it not stay on the tree? Why did it fall to the ground? It's because there is something called gravity, a force by which large bodies attract smaller ones. Hence the apple falls to the ground. Its fall is caused by gravity.

Transfer this to human affairs. Suppose we sought to explain some form of behaviour. Can we use the same notion of cause? Suppose we wish to explain child abuse. There is one explanation that suggests a cycle of abuse, or its intergenerational transmission. Basically, the simple formula would be that if a person was abused as a child then they themselves would become a perpetrator of abuse. Through some mechanisms, being abused as a child 'causes' the person, as an adult, to abuse their own children. There is clear evidence of such a link, but, as you might guess, it's not that simple. This is because we are, in social science, dealing with probability. This means we might well talk in terms of trends or tendencies.

The causal model, when applied to human behaviour, assumes that many factors may contribute to a causal explanation of particular phenomena, even where we haven't fully understood them or even discovered them all. Thus, where we are looking at intergenerational transmission of abuse, factors other than simply being abused as a child may play a part. There may be stresses that the woman experiences: she may live in poverty, and the stress of making ends meet help give her a short fuse; she may be the subject of domestic violence; she may have low self-esteem, making it difficult to form proper affectional bonds with the child.

There may also be factors conferring protection on the mother, despite her past experience of abuse. At the time of the abuse she may have had someone of emotional significance to turn to, helping her cope better, and even encouraging her confidence. She may have other factors in her life at present, such as supportive friends.

All these mean that we will not expect to explain 100 per cent of abuse in terms of the abuse the client suffered as a child. Child abuse is not only a matter of childhood experiences. We cannot expect a 100 per cent correlation between the experience of abuse as children and being an abusive adult. However, we may well find that there is a raised incidence of abuse in families where the mother was herself abused when a child. These women are more likely to be abusers.

What does it mean to say some social phenomenon was caused by something? It means that, say, abuse resulted from something that the person did not themselves control or choose.

Voluntarism is the idea that we undertake actions of our own accord, and that we are therefore responsible for those actions and their consequences. We undertake actions because we choose to do so. Causation is an alternative way of viewing things: they may be the product of forces and factors in the world that you cannot control and may not even recognize. Your actions, in short, may be caused by something.

Deduction and induction – the logic of theory development

One of the more important functions of knowledge development is the development of theory that reflects or organizes the empirical evidence (observations gained from research) in social life.

Theories are attempts to explain particular aspects of the social world by identifying key aspects and delineating the relationship between these aspects. We may look at quality of parenting in terms of self-esteem, past experience, current social support, and so on; we would seek to identify the nature of the relationship between these factors in our explanation. There are two major approaches to theory development:

- one that involves *theory testing*, which is called **deductive theorizing**
- another that involves *theory building*, which is called **inductive theorizing**.

Deductive theorizing

A deductive approach applies a clear process to a problem. Take, for example, the issue of adolescent runaways. With deductive theorizing the researcher begins with a theory, then derives one or more hypotheses from it for testing. For instance, family dysfunctioning may be seen to explain why adolescents run away. A statement is made: adolescent absconding from home occurs where there is general family dysfunctioning.

Next, the researcher defines the variables in each hypothesis and how they should be measured. This would focus on aspects of family functioning, such as style of parenting or interactions between different family members. Hence, the research may focus on a style of parenting as, for example, containing strong disciplinary elements, and a failure to 'listen' to the concerns of the young people. These would be components of family dysfunctioning that we would seek to relate to adolescent absconding.

Finally, the researcher implements the specific measurements. They thus observe the way things really are, and see if their observations confirm, or fail to confirm, the hypothesis. In this case, they would seek to relate a tendency to absconding by adolescents to the presence of a strongly disciplinary parent. We have, then, a theory (that family dysfunctioning causes adolescent absconding), and a process by which this may be tested against evidence that we may collect through research.

One study by Ransford (1968), also quoted in Rubin and Babbie (2001), looked at the Watts riots in Los Angeles. From the literature he found that social isolation and powerlessness were often factors identified with political violence. He felt that these two variables might lie at the bottom of the rioting in Watts. He suggested African Americans who felt powerless would be more likely to riot than black people already participating in mainstream society. His research looked at mainstream social isolation in terms of the extent of contacts and socialization with white people in the community. It focused on powerlessness by attitude scales focusing on the degree to which they could exercise some control over the events. He characterized each person in terms of levels of powerlessness and social isolation. He found those with high social isolation and high powerlessness were more likely to be willing to use violence and to report having done so for political ends.

Inductive theorizing

Social scientists can operate in the opposite direction. They can start with observation of social life (research) and seek to discover patterns that may point to more or less universal principles. They do not start with theory, but seek to explore the social world through research, and then, by analysing findings, try to identify patterns – key aspects, ideas and connections through which they begin to develop theory. Theory is here grounded in empirical research.

Goffman (1961), for example, examined, through observation, behaviour in mental institutions (an example of a 'total institution', like prisons). He developed the idea of spoiled identity – that is the way in which an individual's very sense of identity is spoiled by the process of labelling and incarceration.

Takeuchi's (1974) study, quoted in Rubin and Babbie (2001), of drug use in Hawaii showed similar inductivism. Some had suggested that marijuana use arose because of academic failure. But, starting with this hypothesis, he found no major differences. So he went back to the data. He found that women were less likely to smoke than men, Asians less likely to smoke than non-Asians, and students living at home less likely to smoke than those away from the family home. He began to ask: Why do some people not smoke? At that time, public nonconformist or outrageous behaviour was frowned upon in women. Likewise Asian families were distinguished by their particularly strong adherence to obedience to the law. Those away from home are, of course, less constrained by familial expectations. He theorized that the issue was one of social constraint – that those who did not smoke were more likely to experience social constraints. Hence the theory came out of research findings.

Deductive research is about theory (or hypothesis) testing, while inductive research involves theory development.

Key initial dimensions in the appraisal of research
What should we look for in a piece of social research?

Problem formulation

Problem formulation is the first key thing to develop. A difficulty is recognized, for which more knowledge is needed. We might look, for example, at an issue:

- What part does the peer group play in teenagers becoming involved in criminal behaviour?

- How effective is reminiscence therapy in increasing the morale of older people in residential care?

Each of these is fairly precisely formulated (though not yet properly operationalized). Before we formulated these questions precisely, we would be interested, perhaps, in a particular area: young people becoming lawbreakers; actions taken to improve the morale of older people already in residential care. So what we do is move from an 'area of interest' to the formulation of a question. We might alternatively formulate hypotheses. We might have the hypotheses:

- Young people are more likely to begin criminal behaviour when their peer group is already engaged in such behaviour.

- Older people in residential care experiencing reminiscence therapy will show improved morale to a greater extent than those not receiving this therapy.

Questions and hypotheses represent a more precise formulation of the research problem, enabling the researcher to focus with greater exactitude on their area of interest. So one of the questions for those appraising social research is: Is the research problem formulated clearly and precisely?

Now people can, and do, change the focus of their research some way through. This is particularly the case with inductive and qualitative research, which may start with a more general 'area of interest'. However, we should expect that the researcher is able in their account to identify the research problem with clarity.

> Where inductive approaches are used, they should be able to give an account of the 'journey' travelled to get to the point of the more specific problem formulation. Where deductive approaches are used, there should be clarity and precision at the outset in the delineation of the research problem.

Literature review

This is another important element of the research process. In some ways this sits between the initial identification of an 'area of interest' and the precise formulation of the problem. In the literature review, the researcher is trying to accomplish a number of tasks. Most important is to get an idea of the area. What has been published? What kinds of issues are considered important? How has the knowledge developed over the years – what kind of direction is it going in? In doing this we are able to get to know the area, and formulate themes.

These themes involve both substantive and conceptual areas. For example, when we look at social work or health visiting with child care, there may be a number of substantive areas: child protection, foster care, the 'career' of the child as client, family support, and so on. Each of these begins to delineate areas of research. In fact they will be further subdivided. Child protection could involve looking at: the decision-making processes in child protection; predictive factors for child abuse; the experience of parents undergoing child protection procedures; the quality of partnership in child protection, and so on. Conceptual (or formal) areas will emerge that relate to these. For example, we might have issues such as 'welfare drift', client morale, exclusion or disempowerment. These areas might at times cut across the substantive areas looked at; they represent important 'ways of thinking' in the area of interest. A literature review, therefore, involves:

- becoming acquainted with the substantive interests written about in the area

- looking at some of the formal knowledge used in, or potentially relevant to, the study area.

Another feature is an examination of the methodologies used – that is, the way a researcher goes about identifying and collecting information or data and their assumptions in doing this. There is a range of potential methodologies in any study area. We will go into the more important of these later in the book. Some may be **quantitative** – where, for example, we wish to know how the number of people on the child protection register varies between different local authorities, or we wish to measure outcomes (e.g. whether a particular intervention programme reduces the rate of [re]offending amongst young people). They can also be **qualitative**: How does it feel to be faced with a social worker on your doorstep who is making an enquiry following a child abuse allegation? What are the discourses, or stated ways of making sense of their world, used by social workers in the day-to-day conduct of their practice?

For the person making a critical appraisal of the literature review it is important to be aware if they refer to methodologies. Not all reviews do, but they might do where they wish to argue that a particular methodology has not yet been used, and they wish to argue that such a methodology would throw new light on the matter. This is not about finding a new substantive area, but more about a new approach to looking at a substantive area.

The third key element in appraisal of the literature review is to examine to what extent, or how effectively, the author has made a case for the area they wish to be studied. In this there are certain important questions:

- Is this really a new area, which has not been studied before? Or a new way of focusing on an existing problem?

- How well does this follow the progression of previous research?

- Is this an area for which a convincing case has been made that it is important?

The literature review, therefore, is closely linked to the initial stages of problem formulation, between the original interest in an area, and the precise formulation of problem, hypothesis or question.

The main body of data and conclusion

How we view the main body of data very much depends both on the area of interest identified and the methods used. The methods used are going to be the subject of sustained analysis over the next series of chapters (and they diverge, it should be noted, quite considerably). However, we can look at some issues relating to presentation and analysis. These can perhaps be formulated in terms of the kind of questions that the appraiser may wish to ask.

How clearly has the author presented the methods used and the area studied? Have they given enough information to enable us to judge the quality of the study? One of the most important issues in judging the merit of a study is in relation to methods. Different methods may be used, and these have differing strengths and weaknesses, as well as different assumptions. But without information on how the methods were used in a particular study, it is difficult to judge the quality of data produced. The main paper may look elegant and convincing, but may actually hide rather poor attention to the detail of rigorous use of methods. If, for example, we are trying to track the frequency with which a child manifests tantrums on a week-on-week basis, then it would not be much good doing a retrospective interview after six months. It would be better if we had some sort of diary, in which, for example, the mother was expected to record daily the number of tantrums manifested by the child. But it is not just that. How would tantrums be defined? Is the woman concerned really focusing on what most people would regard as a tantrum – some excessive form of aggressive and defiant behaviour – or does she have a much lower threshold? If it is low, we might have reason to question the data.

However, if we were trying to look at the overall strategy adopted by a practitioner in the conduct of their intervention, picking a six-month period, using retrospective method might be appropriate. We might interview them at six-monthly intervals to view the progression of the case, and of their strategy. Again, however, if it were retrospective, we might be wise to note the possibility of post hoc rationalizing of their actions on the part of the social worker.

> Findings are NEVER straightforward and uncomplicated. We need to be aware of the status of the knowledge we are using.

How well do the findings follow from the problem formulated and methods used? We are here concerned with the way the study focuses on issues of importance from the point of view of problem formulation, and the way the methods have led to the findings. Take, for example, the possibility of using, say, a 72-hour response time as an arbiter of the quality of response to referrals (the kind so beloved of social or health services department managers). We might examine the number of cases that fell in or out of this category and then judge the quality of the response. But does this really help our judgement? If it is the only indicator, it is a pretty poor indicator. What, for example, of the approachability of the health or social worker? Or of the effort they put in to responding? Or of the care they showed? And so on. Furthermore, does it distinguish appropriately between cases? What about referrals made to see an individual discharged from hospital at home, but who won't be home for four days? Or to see clearly non-urgent clients? The methods should not just be appropriate, but be sufficient to examine the issue with which the researcher is concerned.

How far are the conclusions justified by the main body of data? This again is very important. Writers may be tempted to make claims for their data that are not warranted by their findings. For example, we may find one localized study of social workers' responsiveness to child protection referrals. We might have findings that said they were slow, and did not always examine all the salient issues. However, if the author then went on to make general claims about social workers in general (they are careless, they are not sufficiently responsive, their quality of professionalism is in doubt) this is not going to be warranted by such a study. A small study may well reflect only local factors, and these local factors should be identified. At best, we would have to say that such findings give cause for concern, because if they happen in one place they may happen in others. Care, in other words, is required in presentation and appraisal of conclusions.

How far has the author outlined the limits to the study? This is part of the kind of appraisal by the writers themselves of their work. As I have already suggested, there is no such thing as a perfect piece of research. Research can simply make us better informed than we would otherwise be by being more rigorous than we might be in our individual lives, and being able to look more generally and reliably at problems. Thus we would expect to see some commentary on the limits to the methodologies, to findings, and to the generalizability of the findings.

We might, for example, comment on the response rate. If we are taking a sample, what is a sufficient response rate? Is it 95 per cent or 75 per cent? Could it be 50 per cent? How far can we say that we have accurately got the perceptions of even that sample we sought to interview, where not all those who should have been interviewed were interviewed?

What about the geographical area being studied? Is it representative of other areas or the country as a whole? How far does the nature of the area, or type of institution studied, give us good cause to believe that the findings can be generalized to other places or settings? Actually, some researchers, particularly amongst those who use ethnography, do not play up the issue of generalizability. However, from the point of view of professionals wishing to use findings to inform their practice, knowing whether they are relevant to their practice is rather important.

What about the instruments used? How suited were they for the task at hand? For example, we might use a measure of mental illness. Is it always accurate in identifying mental illness, or is it really a screening instrument that gives a probability of identifying mental illness. If it is a screening instrument, are there any implications for the study itself? Does it mean that some people identified as mentally ill or otherwise were misclassified? What are the implications of this for the findings?

These are the kinds of issues with which we can genuinely be concerned when focusing on research reports, in the form of books, articles, theses, and even unpublished reports.

> The reader and user of research may critically appraise that research from a number of points, including problem formulation, literature review, main body of data and conclusion.

From now we should turn in more detail to individual methodologies, and we will first turn to quantitative methods.

Exercises

3.1 Some issues that can be discussed after reading this chapter

- How do we distinguish between research that treats the social world as (a) subjective and (b) objective?
- What distinguishes a voluntaristic perception of humans?
- What is causation? What is probabilistic causation?
- What are the key characteristics of deductive thinking?
- What are the key characteristics of inductive thinking?
- Identify some key areas of interest for those appraising social research.

3.2 An exercise using social research

Examine the following article, or another of your choosing, and consider it in the light of the questions outlined below. This question involves a survey of mental health of the Asian community.

Hatfield, B., Mohammad, H., Rahim, Z. and Tanweer, H. (1996) 'Mental health and the Asian communities: A local survey.' *British Journal of Social Work 26*, 3, 315–337.

1. **Background** – What are the main issues/areas outlined in the literature review? Are there any areas/issues that are absent?

2. **Problem formulation** – What is the main question/ hypothesis in the study? How clearly is the problem formulated? Do the authors adequately demonstrate that the study is original?

3. **Methods** – What are the methods used? Have they given us enough information to judge the quality of the study? What questions are in your mind and what issues are needed to gain

a full account of the method? Is the approach inductive or deductive?

4. **Findings** – Describe the findings of the study. How far are they justified by the evidence presented? Are there any gaps?

5. **Conclusion** – Outline the conclusions made. How far are the conclusions justified by the findings/main body of the data? How far has the author outlined the limits to the study?

6. **Relevance** – What relevance, if any, does the study have for practice?

CHAPTER FOUR
Questionnaire Design for Quantitative Research: Structured Instruments

Questionnaires are available for practitioners to use in their everyday life. We can use them to measure family functioning, parenting style, psychological well-being, and a host of other circumstances. Health visitors have increasingly, for example, used the Edinburgh scale to look at mothers' psychological state in the post-birth period. The Assessment Framework pack, published by the government, for Children in Need and Their Families, contains a pack of questionnaires, or instruments, that may potentially be used by practitioners. Various instruments have been used by psychiatric nurses to help their assessment of mental state and social functioning. The use of these is, as far as we can tell, variable, and there may at times be some reluctance to use them. Nevertheless, they remain a part of the armoury of social and health workers.

For that reason alone, it is a good idea to consider questionnaires and their development. However, questionnaires also provide a crucial building block for quantitative research, and so need to be understood by practitioners who are in the business of making use of such research in their practice.

Quantitative research is research that seeks to ascribe numbers to facets of social life. How many people suffer some form of mental illness in a particular area? What are the rates of petty crime? Do these vary by age, sex or ethnic group? And so on.

At the heart of quantitative social research is the use of questionnaires, or fully structured instruments, which can yield aggregates of numbers when analysed together. For example, we can know how many clients seeking social services support, or patients attending general practice, sought help with practical matters, compared with the number seeking advice, or medical help, or counselling, or some kind of resources, such as access to a day centre or residential home. We do this by asking them why they got in contact with social services or general practice, and give them a range of possible responses (this is not the only way of doing things – there are, for example, open questions – of which more later) from which they identify the one that is most accurate for them. Thus we could ask the questions *Why did you get in contact with social services?* or *Why did you attend general practice?* and the available responses would be:

Counselling	☐
Advice	☐
Practical help	☐
Day/residential care	☐
Medical help	☐
Other (state)	☐

In general, people might be asked to tick one of the boxes for all these. In that case, you might get (say for an elderly client group, numbering 100) the following results:

Counselling	5
Advice	10
Practical help	35
Day/residential care	20
Medical help	20
Other	10
Total	100

Because the number of each of these is a proportion of 100, each of these represents a percentage. Thus, we can deduce that 35 per cent wanted practical help – this was most frequently requested – while at the other end counselling was only sought on 5 per cent of occasions. We know which was the most frequently sought, which was the least frequently sought, and all points between. The use of this information is obvious where, for example, we are seeking to plan social services or GP provision.

What we see here, in a simple example, is the link between the individual questionnaire and the results that emerge when findings taken from a whole group are aggregated. It is generally for this kind of aggregating purposes that questionnaires are produced.

Now, of course, this assumes two things:

- that each item (counselling, advice, etc.) has only a yes/no alternative
- that the person completing the form could respond yes to only one item.

If either of these were changed the results would differ. For example, if the respondent could answer yes to more than one item, the total responses would amount to more than 100, while the number of respondents (people asked) would still only be 100. So we could get an individual questionnaire ticked/crossed as follows:

Counselling	☒
Advice	☐
Practical help	☐
Day/residential care	☒
Medical help	☐
Other (state)	☐

And we could have results (for a different group of 100) as follows:

Counselling	26
Advice	25
Practical help	45
Day/residential care	30
Medical help	35
Other (state)	40

The total responses would then be 201, but the number of respondents would remain 100.

This gives a basic idea of the way the questionnaire framing affects results. In both the first and second case practical help was the most frequently sought, but the least frequently sought was different (counselling in the first and advice in the second). Clearly we need to pay attention to questionnaire design when seeking to interpret findings from quantitative studies using questionnaires.

The function and purpose of questionnaires

Oppenheim (1992) suggests that the function of the questionnaire is measurement. We seek to measure, on an individual level, what it is that the individual wants, what their views are, or some facets of their situation. Thus, at an individual level, we know an individual wanted residential and day care, but not advice. This measure, so to speak, is 1–0 to residential and day care versus counselling! More important is the way it fits with aggregation: questionnaires provide the basis for identifying, with any particular group, the frequency with which any particular item is sought, preferred or viewed, and does so (often) in comparison with alternative items.

Some questionnaires are designed to be used both for individuals and social research. One such instrument I have used a lot is the Beck Depression Inventory, which at the individual level yields a total score indicating whether a person is clinically depressed, but which can also be used, in social research, to identify, for example, the frequency of depression in a particular population group (such as a local population, or attendees at surgery, or family centre members, etc.).

A questionnaire seeks to provide a standard format (i.e. one precisely the same for all respondents) on which facts, comments and attitudes can be recorded. Thus we would present all respondents with the same alternative items, and in the same order, so that we can get results about why they got in contact with social or health services.

Questionnaires allow us to enumerate. They provide us with information through which we can determine the scale of any particular thing that we like to look at. We may know, from asking people anecdotally, that they are concerned about the level of crime. However, we don't know how many people think that the level of crime is a major concern for them, and we also don't know for what proportion of the population this is the case. Standardized questionnaires allow us to gain such information.

There are various processes through which social researchers would be expected to go in order to develop a rigorous questionnaire. It is useful to consider whether this has happened when examining the validity with which books and articles produce findings based on questionnaires.

> The function of the questionnaire is measurement, and this is achieved through a standard format for recording facts, comments and attitudes.

Question:　What particular help for practice is provided by enumeration?

The process of questionnaire development

While we have summarized some key general issues for questionnaires, there is also the particular question of the specific function of the questionnaire within a particular research project. A questionnaire is always developed in relation to a particular overall research plan, and particular objectives or questions. What is the relationship between the plan or objectives and the instrument produced? The starting point may be one that draws upon a proper conceptual understanding of the area, or which draws upon some empirical understanding of the ways in which it is viewed by the target population, through which an appropriate type and range of items can be derived.

Conceptual understanding

Let us take an example from my own work, an important issue within child care social work, but also relevant for health professionals such as health visitors: the quality of partnership with parents (Sheppard 2001). If we were interested in the question 'What is the quality of partnership between social worker (or indeed health professionals) and mother in child care cases?', we would seek to develop a questionnaire that reflected this central concern. We would wish to find the main elements of partnership and to find ways of expressing them so that they could be measured. How do we do this?

It was important to explore, first of all, what is meant by the concept 'partnership'. This is not a straightforward thing. If we look at official publications (e.g. Department of Health 1995), we find a wide variety of definitions that are not particularly rigorous, and often not consistent with each other. If one looks at practice, we find things even more unclear. Practitioners have only the vaguest idea of what is being talked about, and at times are quite cynical. How, they ask, are we to be in partnership where child protection is involved? Such situations are often characterized by conflict (inimical to partnership) and the use of authority (inimical to the implicit equality involved in partnership). It was, therefore, necessary to do three things:

- examine the underlying assumptions of partnership, which allowed us to give it some 'content'

- identify some of the practical dimensions of it as a concept (e.g. the issue of involvement in decision making, expectations of who should do what, and so on)

- find a way to operationalize these elements.

This third point means making these elements into statements that could be used in the real-world situation of the use of the questionnaire.

This led to the development of a number of key dimensions, through which we could assess the quality of partnership. First, we were able to identify some core conceptual elements (notions of role, role relationship and empowerment); then the key dimensions (partnership morale, active involvement, and consultation and decision making). From this we developed operationalized items or statements that would be used in the study. These included measuring the woman's sense of energy, motivation and confidence; participation in decision making and involvement in decision implementation; and consultation and receipt of information.

Through this process we were able to begin to move from the vague statements about partnership that came from government and practice, to a set of dimensions and operationalized items that would provide the basis for the questionnaire.

So we have:

1. the central focus of the research and its objectives

2. conceptualization of key issues in relation to the central focus and objectives

3. identifying the main domains which make up these key issues and which should therefore be measured

4. operationalizing these by identifying a number of items which could be presented to the respondent.

This is far from the whole process, as we shall see, but it provides the first stages of developing a questionnaire.

Question: Are the conceptual dimensions of questionnaires
                 relevant for practice?

Empirically developed instruments

Instruments can be empirically based in two ways:

- They can draw upon existing research through which the
  major dimensions may be identified.

- They can be based on the development of domains and items
  that emerge from initial research done by the person who
  develops the questionnaire.

One example from social work of the former is the Social Assessment
Schedule (SAS) and Parent Concerns Questionnaire, which I have developed (Sheppard 1999; Sheppard and Watkins 2000). This is an instrument to identify the psychosocial problems associated with depression
in families subject to child and family care. It was developed by examining the main parameters of problems that had been found by a wide
range of existing research to be associated with depression. Amongst
the key dimensions were various social and material problems, such as
housing, financial and home management problems. Also there were social and relationship problems, health problems, and parenting and
child care problems. On the basis of the research the main dimensions of
the instrument were developed, reflecting these broad problem areas.

Others have sought to identify key areas through carrying out initial
research. This is the case with Goldberg and Wharburton's (1979) *Ends
and Means in Social Work* – their case review schedule. In this case, they
sought to identify the key elements of problems and of intervention
types by examining case records, through which the major domains
could be identified. These included issues like basic information on case
status and demographic information, problem areas and intervention
forms.

In the case of the SAS, it was not simply the main domains that were
identified, but further work formulating the detailed items was under-

taken with a group of social workers themselves, so that the items were framed in a way immediately understandable to a social work audience. They reflected, to use a technical term, 'occupational meanings'.

A key point here, then, in examining any questionnaire developed, is to ask: What is the process by which the main dimensions and items in the questionnaire was developed? Did the developer seek to conceptualize the central concerns in the right way, and how far did they go through an appropriate process to develop the main items?

In principle we should seek to cover the area comprehensively, by identifying all the elements and operationalizing them in the items incorporated into the instrument. Questionnaires should be developed from a clear conceptual or empirical (evidence) base, from which the details of the questionnaire may be developed. However, it will not always be the case that those who develop questionnaires go through this kind of process. To the extent that they do not, there is a problem.

Take, for example, a situation where the range of items is simply dreamed up by someone, without any reference either to some conceptual understanding of the issue, or to some clear empirical basis (e.g. initial interviews, through which the main dimension can be identified). This creates the possibility of serious flaws in the instrument:

- It may well not be comprehensive, or at least not cover the main dimensions of any issue with which they are concerned.
- Second, it may have little relevance to the population groups with which they are concerned. We may, in other words, be looking at entirely the wrong kind of thing.

Formulation of questionnaire items
Types of question
There are three basic ways in which individual items may be formed:

- binary choice questions
- multiple choice questions
- scales.

BINARY CHOICE

We may first have what amounts to simple yes/no questions. They can be presented in terms of yes or no, or, for example, by requiring a tick. This would be the case with the following:

Are you married?   YES / NO
(Please circle the correct answer)

OR

Gender   Male   ☐
            Female   ☐

MULTIPLE CHOICE

Here the respondent is asked to choose between several alternative statements. The intention is that they identify that which most accurately describes their state or situation. From the Beck Depression Inventory (Beck, Steer and Garbin 1988) we have:

a. I do not feel sad.   ☐
b. I feel sad.   ☐
c. I am sad all the time and I can't snap out of it.   ☐
d. I am so sad or unhappy that I can't stand it.   ☐

This is clearly a set of statements indicating ever greater levels or depths of the condition with which it is concerned – sadness.

SCALES

Scales involve the respondent making a judgement about the extent to which they 'fit' with a statement. For example, the respondent might be asked to rate the severity of a particular problem. In the Family Problem Questionnaire used in Jane Gibbons's (1990) research on family support, they had items such as (a) family problems (b) need for practical advice:

Our family is facing a lot of problems at the moment	2	1	0	−1	−2
We need advice about how to get welfare benefits we are entitled to	2	1	0	−1	−2

where 2= strongly agree, 1= agree, 0= uncertain, −1= disagree, −2= strongly disagree

In these cases the respondent is asked to rate the severity of these problems by identifying the extent to which they agree or disagree with them. From the Social Assessment Schedule (SAS) we have a scale that does not involve negatives or minus numbers:

	Present	Severe
Lack of Relationships (persistent isolation/limited social network)	☐	☐

Here we have three dimensions: (a) not present (don't tick), (b) present, (c) severe.

Examples of scales used in health and social work research

LIKERT SCALES

In Likert scales, the respondent is not asked simply whether they agree or disagree with a statement/item, but to choose between several response categories identifying the extent of agreement or disagreement. An example of a Likert scale is the Family Problem Questionnaire, above. The respondent's attitude is measured by the total score achieved in the questionnaire. Of course, where properly constructed, they can provide scores for individual elements of the questionnaire.

SEMANTIC DIFFERENTIAL SCALES

This is where a number of opposite adjectives are presented in relation to a particular concept (e.g. socialism). There are a number of spaces/locations between the two extremes and respondents are invited to identify where they place themselves.

GOOD	_____	BAD
KIND	_____	CRUEL
TRUE	_____	FALSE

Types of measurement

Scales, or measures, are generally divided into different types as follows:

- nominal measures
- ordinal measures
- interval measures
- ratio measures.

NOMINAL MEASURES

There should be at least two categories, and they should be distinct, mutually exclusive and exhaustive. For example, sex – there are two categories, they are distinct and mutually exclusive, and they cover all possibilities. This is really a way of classifying.

ORDINAL MEASURES

These too consist of mutually exclusive categories. However, categories are ranked in order of their value. So we could be saying that people regard having a home as more important than a refrigerator, which in turn is more important than a vacuum cleaner. Hence they would have the rank:

1. House

2. Refrigerator

3. Vacuum cleaner

INTERVAL MEASURES

These are the same as ordinal measures, except you have the same 'distance' between measures. For example we might measure social work intervention length in terms of weeks. We know that one week is as long as another – hence the 'interval' between each measure is the same. There are few examples of interval scales in the social sciences that are not also ratio scales (see below). The best example is that of an Intelligence Quotient (IQ) test. While IQ scores are interval data, they do not in any meaningful sense have a zero score because of the manner of calculation (see Black 1999).

RATIO MEASURES

Ratio measures have the same properties as interval measures but also have an absolute zero. So we can measure ratio. This would be the case with number of visits to a client. We would know, for example, that 13 interviews are 13 times as many as one interview.

Appraising comprehensiveness and efficiency

Once we have established that the questionnaire is – at least at face value and in terms of items – being constructed in terms of the particular research issue or problem (and not some other issue through lack of clarity about research problem or objectives), we then have to look at the extent to which it covers all the areas relevant to the research problem. If, for example, we are interested in partnership with parents, do we have the range of items that will give us a sufficiently comprehensive picture of the situation regarding partnership? The same goes for social functioning – does a questionnaire on social functioning cover the key areas sufficiently comprehensively?

However, a spanner in the works is created by the need to keep the attention of the respondent. There is no point in having a questionnaire that is so long that the respondent loses interest and gives perfunctory or inaccurate answers, or simply refuses to complete it. This is particularly the case where there is more than one instrument involved. Where, for example, we are looking at the relationship between the presence of depression in mother, child care problems and the coping strategy in dealing with those problems, then you have three questionnaires to complete. It follows that we need to complement comprehensiveness with efficiency – achieving the widest possible coverage of items in the most limited 'space' possible.

Take the Social Assessment Schedule (SAS). We are interested here in identifying the range of problems confronted by social workers in child care, but in a way that does not overload them when they are busy in the direct tasks of working with clients. We can look at the domain of child problems, and focus on 'child emotional problems' (one of a whole variety of child problems identified). Now child emotional problems can clearly be applied to all ages, but they will be likely to manifest themselves in different ways. Thus we may have persistent crying in a 9-month-old, bed wetting in a 7-year-old, violent behaviour in an 11-year-old, or depression in a 15-year-old. All these could be included, as well as others, as specific aspects of emotional problems in different age groups. However, we would quickly be overloaded by the range and number of problems, and in all likelihood social workers would refuse to fill them in. Expansion of items would be self-defeating.

Likewise in the SAS, we could develop a questionnaire that separately examined the problems of every individual child in the family (the SAS focuses on data in relation to all children in the family). However, the focus of the research was on depressed mothers, so, while it might be interesting, balancing the advantages of more information against the disadvantages of increasing the research 'workload' on respondents, this would not have been an efficient approach to the research.

This gets to the heart of comprehensiveness. It needs to be sufficient for the purposes of presenting coherent findings that give a picture of what is going on in relation to the research question, without overloading or 'turning off' the respondents and making the researcher's task of gathering information impossible.

Questionnaires should ideally be as comprehensive as possible, but short enough to be efficient and usable in research.

Standardizing

There is a crucial assumption in questionnaires, particularly those involving closed questions, that respondents should be given 'equivalence of stimulus'. This means that respondents are expected to experience and understand the questionnaire in the same way as all other respondents receiving the questionnaire. If I ask you one particular question, or make one particular statement, it must mean exactly the same to you as it does to me, as it does to anyone else who receives the questionnaire.

Standardizing the interview

We are aiming with the questionnaire, to approach as near as possible, the notion that every respondent has been asked:

- the same question
- with the same meaning
- with the same intonation (if through an interview)
- in the same sequence.

Thus, when we look at our statistical results and find, for example, that significantly more women than men said 'yes' to a particular question, we want to be sure that we are dealing with a genuine sex difference, and not an interviewer effect, or an artefact of the instrument. An interviewer effect would be that the interviewer administered the questionnaire in such a way that it biased the answers they got. An artefact of the questionnaire would be one where the questionnaire itself was phrased or ordered in such a way that it created a bias between different groups studied.

This could happen, for example, where particularly personal questions were being asked. Say, for example, the questionnaire was asking particularly personal aspects of sexual behaviour, and that both men and women were being interviewed by a man, we might have reason to believe that the women might feel uncomfortable responding to such questions to a male stranger. They might be less forthright than they would be if there was a female interviewer. Major differences, then, might reflect genuine differences between men and women, but they also might reflect the possibility that women were less forthright. Under these circumstances there would be an 'interviewer effect'.

The same could be said about the issue of 'outsider' and 'insider'. Where, for example, social workers were being interviewed, they might regard a researcher who has 'been there, done that' as more likely to be fair in reporting findings than a researcher who has no such background. The trust, sense of identity and rapport that it is possible to build up with an insider can make respondents more confident that they can be honest in their responses.

So, it can be helpful to know who the interviewer is, and to make an appraisal of findings in the light of this.

Question: What, if anything, might practitioners learn from 'interviewer effect'?

Standardization of questionnaires

In pursuit of standardization, books on research methods identify a whole range of dos and don'ts in relation to questionnaire construction. Some of the more frequently encountered are:

• Ask specific questions.

• Use simple language.

• Avoid ambiguity.

• Don't always expect accurate recall.

QUESTIONS SHOULD BE SPECIFIC (OR NOT INSUFFICIENTLY SPECIFIC)

One of the problems is where two questions are asked in one. If you are interested in parents' involvement in decision making as an aspect of partnership, you should not simply ask:

How satisfied were you with involvement in decision making?

Rather you should first ask:

To what extent were you involved in decision making?

Then:

How satisfied were you with involvement in decision making?

Here we must be aware that different parents may want different levels of involvement in decision making. Some may want little, others may want a lot. The point is they could actually be dissatisfied if they are involved too much, where they do not want this to be the case. They may feel pressured by the social worker. Thus we should not assume that all parents wish to be as involved as each other, and that therefore satisfaction will be related to this, unless we are able to demonstrate such a connection.

Likewise, a general question 'How far were you involved in partnership?' (with answers: a great deal, to some extent, not very much) would rather gloss over the detailed elements of partnership.

SIMPLE LANGUAGE

In choosing the language for a questionnaire, the population studied should be kept in mind. The aim of the wording is to communicate with respondents as close as possible to their own language, in a relatively straghtforward and jargon-free way. Technical language in particular is to be avoided in the general population. However, when surveying a profession, it is acceptable to use technical language, as long as it is in wide use and similarly understood by respondents.

Questionnaire designers should put themselves in the position of the typical population group they are surveying. Generally it is advisable that questionnaires should use the simplest terms that will convey the exact meaning.

AMBIGUITY

Ambiguous questions are to be avoided at all costs. If ambiguity creeps in, different people will understand the question differently and hence will, in effect, be answering different questions. For example:

> Is caring for your children more difficult because you are expecting a baby?

If this is said to all women irrespective of whether they are expecting, what does NO mean? It could mean:

> No, I'm not expecting a baby.

or

> No, it's not more difficult.

QUESTIONS INVOLVING MEMORY

Many questions involve respondents using some kind of recall. However, questionnaires should seek to avoid asking questions where accurate recall may be difficult to achieve. Two factors are of importance here:

- the length of time since an event took place
- the importance of the event to the respondent.

If you were asked what you were doing on 23 July 1999, you may well have no idea. On the other hand, we know that events involving trauma (post-traumatic stress disorder) can be vividly and accurately remembered years after the event. Likewise, landmark events can be clearly remembered. Most people who were alive at the time can remember where they were on the day Kennedy was assassinated, or (in Eritain) when Margaret Thatcher resigned.

Reliability and validity

Once we have developed instruments that have been properly formulated and standardized, once we know the language is appropriate and the instrument is sufficiently comprehensive, and so on, we would expect to examine it for reliability and validity. What do these involve?

Reliability

Reliability means consistency. We have to be sure, as far as possible, that an instrument would perform in the same way with the same people if they encounter the same conditions. Any inconsistency and we would not know that the results derived from the instrument were not down to the collective 'whims of the moment' of respondents. We need to gain some degree of objectivity. For example, using an objectively reliable instrument to detect change over time, we can be fairly sure that changes in ratings represent real changes, and are not the result of some inconsistency arising from the instrument.

However, it is obviously the case that we cannot get perfect consistency. Life is not like that. What we would look for is high levels of consistency. Reliability involves, therefore:

* the reliability of the instrument

* the conditions under which it is used.

Correlation coefficient is the usual way of expressing reliability. It is perhaps beyond the scope of this book to examine in detail the manner by which correlation coefficient is calculated. However, it is rare for it to be above 0.9, and begins to approach unreliability the further below 0.8 it goes (with 1 being perfect reliability or complete consistency).

How is this done?

* Repeat administration of the instrument (test/retest) – the same test is given to the same participants some time later, and the results compared.

- Internal consistency (between variables) using Chronbach's alpha (a technical method, which is beyond the scope of an introductory text, and should not concern the reader).

- Split-half method – the instrument is divided into two and the answers to similar questions in the two halves are compared for consistency.

- Inter-rater reliability – two interviewers, present at the same interview, make ratings on the same instrument which are subsequently compared for their consistency.

Validity

In principle validity indicates the degree to which an instrument measures what it purports to measure (e.g. a partnership instrument measures partnership and not something else). There are four forms of validity:

- face validity
- construct validity
- concurrent validity
- predictive validity.

FACE VALIDITY

Face validity is the basic form. This involves ensuring that the items used fulfil key dimensions of what they should in terms of theoretical criteria or some expert judgement. Does an instrument, for example, measuring need, or social functioning, or psychological well-being, seem to cover the main areas, when examined by experts?

CONSTRUCT VALIDITY

Here we make predictions on good theoretical grounds. We can, for example, see if relationships between similar areas of life are closely associated (e.g. that someone who scores highly on an IQ test will score highly on an arithmetic test).

CONCURRENT VALIDITY

Here we correlate scores with some external criterion (e.g. we would expect higher child problem scores on the SAS to be associated with depression).

PREDICTIVE VALIDITY

Here we focus on the efficacy of the measure in making predictions. For example, we may suggest that women with low social support for child care will have greater child care problems in the future.

None of these give us certainty, but they give us good reason to believe that the instrument is measuring what it purports to measure. In other words, because the instrument seems, in practice, to be operating in the kinds of ways which we would expect, and would seem reasonable, we would consider the instrument to have high levels of validity.

> The testing of reliability and validity are means by which we can ascertain whether a questionnaire is measuring what it purports to measure and whether it is doing it in the same way at different times and with different people.

Overall critique

Although there is a whole set of criteria to which researchers are expected to conform, these kinds of approaches to questionnaires, and the questionnaires themselves, have been subject to criticism from those who feel they are not appropriate to the examination of social life, or that they cannot achieve what they claim to achieve, thus inevitably distorting social life in the presentation of findings.

Some have criticized the questionnaire because, despite its complicated rules, its development implies the possibility of neutral presentation of the social world, in a way that can be agreed by everyone. This is at the heart of getting at the identification of items that 'mean the same to all respondents', and of reliability and validity in use of the questionnaires, which, in effect, *collect facts about the social environment.* However, while we may all agree with the movement of physical objects such as a thermometer, the social world is more complex, and we may well not agree on the nature of what is happening, given even the most carefully developed items in a questionnaire.

Critics have suggested this aim is wrong-headed in principle as well as unattainable in practice. There is a fallacy in it that all people can experience the same question/input in exactly the same way, whereas people bring with them to any situation their own personal backgrounds and understanding of the world, which means they will see things differently. Under such circumstances, standardizing questions is one sure way to make sure that it is perceived by people differently. What is needed is a form of information gathering that pays proper attention to the differences of understanding and meaning that will be manifested by each respondent. This will not be provided by standardized, or fully structured, questionnaires, but rather by more detailed, longer interviews that ask general questions, which can be answered by the subject in their own way, and which allow exploration of their views in more detail.

Another criticism relates to *the interview, and interview context itself.* This is basically an interaction between two people. Critics would see this situation as essentially interactive and subjective. Any answer can only be understood if we know how the respondent felt about the interviewer, about how they felt about being interviewed, about the topic under consideration, and the particular way it was perceived at that particular moment. Indeed, the interview would be seen as a particular context: where two people are playing out roles (those of interviewer and interviewee), where they bring assumptions of the expectations that should be made of them (what kind of thing do I do when I am being interviewed?). Furthermore, different individuals may see these roles in different, sometimes subtly different, ways. These expectations will affect the kinds of responses they might get.

Thus attempts at creating a standardized situation would be regarded by some as 'scientizing' (creating the spurious impression of being scientific), distorting the real nature of what is going on.

However, we can equally well state that these arguments go too far. We may, for example, argue that in a world of shared meanings it is possible to develop items that have similar meanings to all respondents, provided we are careful to ensure only those who share those meanings (some distinct cultural group) are the subject of the study. Indeed, regardless of what theoretical criticisms are made, does not the reliability and validity study demonstrate this to be the case?

This also emphasizes that it is possible to make sure that the questionnaire is developed taking into account the meanings respondents attribute to things – the way they understand their world – rather than developing it with no reference to their understanding.

Finally, there is no reason that we cannot see questionnaires developed in relation to some theory. This must be the case with questionnaires relating to attachment (attachment theory). In this case the questionnaires would be testing that theory by some deductive process, derived from some hypotheses or propositions.

Exercises

4.1 Some issues that can be discussed after reading this chapter

- Describe the general purpose of questionnaires.
- Identify the conceptual and empirical base for questionnaire development.
- What are the different ways of formulating items in a questionnaire?
- What kinds of scales and types of measurement may be used in a questionnaire?
- Identify key factors in the process of standardizing questionnaires and interviews.

- What are reliability and validity? Describe their importance for questionnaire development.
- What criticisms may be made of the use of questionnaires for research?

4.2 An exercise using questionnaires

Look at one of the following:

Claire, A. and Cairns, V. (1978) 'Design, development and use of a standardised interview to assess social maladjustment and dysfunction in community studies.' *Psychological Medicine 8*, 589–604.

Sheppard, M. (2001) 'The design and development of an instrument for assessing the quality of partnership between mother and social worker in child and family care.' *Child and Family Social Work 6*, 1, 31–46.

Other examples from below could substitute, as appropriate, for these papers. Consider the paper in the light of expectations of rigorous practice in the development of questionnaires. Focus should include:

- the conceptual basis of the questionnaire
- empirical evidence as the basis for the questionnaire and its form
- how these relate to the main domains or items in the questionnaire
- efforts made to standardize items and ensure they are understandable to those using it
- efforts to ensure reliability and validity
- limits to the use of, and criticism of, the questionnaire and its practical application.

NB. Do not get hamstrung by the statistics if you find them difficult. Concentrate on the narrative, and the extent to which the development of the questionnaire follows the kinds of procedures it should.

Examples of questionnaire development

Cory, M., Morrison-Brady, D. and Johnson, B. (1997)' The HIV knowledge questionnaire: Development and evaluation of a reliable, valid and practical self administered questionnaire.' *AIDS and Behavior 1*, 1, 61–74.

Hiidenhoui, H., Lappala, P. and Nojone, K. (2001) 'Development of a patient oriented instrument to measure service quality in out patient departments.' *Journal of Advanced Nursing 34*, 5, 696–705.

Hyland, M., Lewith, G. and Westoby, C. (2003) 'Developing a measure of attitudes: The holistic complementary and alternative medicine questionnaire.' *Complementary Therapies in Medicine 11*, 1, 33–38.

Sheppard, M. and Watkins, M. (2000) 'The Parent Concerns Questionnaire: Evaluation of a mothers' self report instrument for the identification of problems and needs in child and family social work.' *Children and Society 14*, 194–206.

Sitzia, J. and Wood, M. (1999) 'Development and evaluation of a questionnaire to assess patient satisfaction with chemotherapy nursing care.' *European Journal of Oncology Nursing 3*, 3, 126–142.

Further reading

Aiken, L. (1997) *Questionnaires and Inventories*. Chichester: Wiley.

Black, T. (1999) *Doing Quantitative Research in the Social Sciences, Part 2*. Thousand Oaks, CA: Sage.

Hammersley, M. and Atkinson, P. (1992) *Ethnography – Principles in Practice*. London: Routledge. (Chapter 1 contains criticism of quantitative questionnaires.)

Mead, D. (1993) 'Personal experience of designing questionnaires.' *Nurse Researcher 1*, 2, 62–70.

Oppenheim, A.N. (1992) *Questionnaire Design, Interviewing and Attitude Measurement*. London: Printer Publishers.

Rubin, A. and Babbie, E. (2001) *Research Methods for Social Work* (4th edn). Belmont, CA: Wadsworth/Thomson.

CHAPTER FIVE
Surveys and Sampling

Right at the beginning of the book we looked at the circumstances in which surveys may be useful for practice. The reader may remember that we referred to the use of surveys in relation to the better understanding of the needs of minority ethnic groups. The example drew attention to the importance of survey research findings to the conduct of practice. In this chapter, we shall explore in more detail the nature and importance of surveys.

Surveys are closely related to questionnaires. Surveys seek to obtain information about particular population groups, normally in a manner that will allow us to quantify their responses. The quantification is of considerable importance. In principle, it allows us to give a certain 'weighting' to particular facets of a population in which we are interested, or to weigh up different views or attitudes.

In the social work and health professions we might, for example, wish to know about:

- people's views about community care policies for the mentally ill, specifically placing those formerly long-term patients in psychiatric hospital in the community
- mothers' views about the adequacy of facilities for supporting parents of children under five
- the needs of older people living in the community.

The population refers to the group we are interested in: in these cases we are concerned (a) with the general population, (b) with mothers of children aged under five and (c) people aged over 65. It is clear also that quantification of findings can be useful. We would (being quite simplistic to start with) be interested in knowing, for example, how many people are in favour of placing long-term psychiatric patients in the community, and how many are against it.

If we are able to construct a survey that is representative of the general population, then we would have particularly useful information, since we would be able to infer from this that the population as a whole holds the views we have discovered using the survey. We might, for example, find that 25 per cent were for this policy, 55 per cent against, and 20 per cent 'don't know'. We would know that we should expect considerable opposition to this policy of relocating these patients in the community. This might suggest, for example, that a health or local authority should be strongly proactive in re-educating the community to change their stereotypes of mentally ill people, in order that they would become more accepting. Such a process might be vital for the success of a policy.

What we see here is the importance of surveys in providing information and doing so (normally) numerically/quantitatively, as well as doing it in a way (from a health and social work perspective) that may aid policy and practice. Of course surveys can be carried out which do not affect practice, but social workers would be particularly concerned with the practice aspect.

Surveys are closely related to questionnaires, because questionnaires provide the individualized information from those who have been surveyed. We would use the alternative or multiple-choice questions to get individual information, which is aggregated to provide data for the survey population as a whole.

Overall, then, surveys are used to discover attitudes, perceptions and facts about particular population groups (e.g. the general population's perceptions about violent crime), as well as particular groups, such as the Bangladeshi community.

What should we look for in surveys?

Properly conducted surveys should have certain characteristics:

- They should have a clearly stated research goal (see below).
- They should always carefully define the target population from which information was sought (e.g. we might be examining the experience of racism in child health service provision by the African Caribbean adult population). We would then be targeting (a) African Caribbeans (b) who are aged over 18 and (c) who have used child health services provision. If, for example, we leave out (c) then we may be getting ill-informed views, from people who have little direct experience of the provision, which could then give us misleading results.

- They should identify a sampling frame that describes precisely how the target population has been selected. If, for example, we are surveying the African Caribbean community, but we are not surveying all of them (i.e. we have taken a sample), we need to know exactly how they have been chosen.

- They should specify the data collection methods – for example, was it done by telephone, face-to-face interview, or by post? This should include details of the ways this operated, and any ways in which things fell down compared with the way they had been envisaged in the first place.

- Data collection procedures should be specified to ensure that the quality of data provided was adequate. For example, what did they do if a respondent refused to be interviewed? Who

did they choose next? How did they make sure that the
people who should be included were included?

All the above should be clearly spelled out in the report, in order that we
can judge the quality of the survey (and hence its usefulness).

The research goal

As with all research, the goal, or goals, of research are essential as the
prerequisite to setting up and conducting the survey.

The goal may be *to test a hypothesis.* We could, for example, propose:
Women will view more positively than men the idea that free nursery
and pre-school facilities should be available for low-income families
with children under five.

The goal may be *to test a causal, multivariate model* (this is a model
seeking to explain something that has a number of elements). We might
seek, for example, to discover the relationship between conventional
values, drug use and friendship networks. Here we have a number of related hypotheses:

- People with conventional values are less likely to have ever
  used illegal drugs.
- People with drug-using friends are more likely themselves to
  have used illegal drugs.
- People with conventional values are less likely to have
  drug-using friends.

The goal may be *to identify the percentage of people who hold certain beliefs.*
For example, we might want to discover the proportion of the population that believes that our criminal justice system is working well.

A clearly stated research goal determines the next issue: Who or what
should be the population of interest? We have already seen, for example,
that if we are interested in African Caribbean adults' experience of racism in social services, it is to the actual users that we should turn. If, for
example, we were to survey the general population (in which the major-

ity were not service users), most would not know anything directly, and replies may reflect hearsay, prejudice or merely a desire to respond – not a lot of use when we wish to frame a response based on informed views. Who, in other words, is the survey supposed to represent?

Representativeness and sampling

Is the study representative?

This issue of **representativeness** is one we will come to again. It is, however, central to the value of the survey. This relates to the question: Who is it that is chosen to participate? The source of people who could participate is called the **sampling frame**. For example, we might use the electoral register as a sampling frame if we wish to undertake a general population study of attitudes to crime. We might also use the telephone directory. However, if we are seeking to discover hospital service users' views of the need for a social work service in a hospital, it would not be much use going to the electoral register, as we don't know all who have used the hospital services.

An important question, therefore, is: How well does the sampling frame represent the population we are studying? This is particularly significant in social work. Very often, we are seeking information about social services practice, social work outcomes, social service users and so on. Thus we might be interested in questions like:

- Who uses family centres and what do they use them for? How far does this reflect a successful implementation of family support policy by targeting appropriate need groups?

- What are the main methods of intervention used by social workers in supporting mentally ill patients in the community? Do these vary according to different types of mental health groups? Are they distinctive from, say, community psychiatric nurses?

- How adequate do parents of children with learning
  difficulties perceive services available to them to be?

The question for us is: What do we use as the sampling frame? In general, for example, we find that studies of family centres are single-centre studies or look at a number of centres. But, to what extent can they be considered representative of family centres as a whole? This is extremely problematic. They are generally chosen because of their availability. That is, they can be easily accessed, because (a) they are not too far away to be researched, (b) the family centre workers/managers just happen to be prepared to allow researchers in, and (c) there is sufficient money/resources for the researcher so that it is feasible for the researcher to carry out the research (Cigno 1988; Cigno and Gore 1999; Fells and de Gruchy 1991; Gibbons 1990; Smith 1996). Now, none of these criteria indicate that the family centre or centres studied are in any way representative of *all* family centres in England or Britain (let alone other countries such as the United States). This raises the question of whether any findings are of any general use at all. If it is possible that they are not representative (and this is very possible) the findings may actually be misleading.

Indeed, this is further emphasized by the very diverse nature of family centres. Some are run by local authorities, while others are run by voluntary organizations. The way they are run and managed, and their target population, can all be quite different according to who it is that runs them. Likewise the functions of these centres can vary greatly. Some might have a child protection focus. Others may have a therapeutic parenting skills focus. Still others may be primarily drop-ins for social purposes. Still others may involve all three. What are we to conclude about these family centres?

This kind of approach was taken by Smith (1996), when she looked at family centres. Those that she picked all happened to be run by the National Children's Homes, and they were in diverse areas, and of diverse types. In terms of statistical representativeness (and this is not the only way we can identify representativeness) we have no idea how typical they were.

Even if we are to focus on one type (and we have first of all to determine the main types of family centre), how do we know that the ones we are studying are representative of all the family centres of this type? Very often we don't.

However, we should note at this point that at times it is not statistical representativeness that is being used in health or social work research. We may justify our focus on particular facilities because they represent that kind of facility in general (e.g. a social services child care team) because they have a number of typical characteristics. We might argue that their functions are very similar, that they are organized on lines typical of other child care teams, that those involved are typically qualified in the same way that other teams are (so, for example, a team studied that did not possess a majority of qualified workers would not be typical, and so on). This involves having *representative characteristics* that are typical, rather than being statistically representative. This can be quite convincing, as with my study of social work practice with depressed mothers (Sheppard 2001). The combination of (a) representative characteristics (typical of such teams) and (b) diversity (the three areas studied were in quite different areas, with little obvious 'contamination' of each other by having contact that could influence each other) made the findings strong and convincing, in terms of representativeness.

One way researchers get round this problem is by focusing on pathfinding projects – sort of experiments (in a lay/loose sense) in which something new is being tried out. They become single cases, but cases that others may be interested in, and be interested in duplicating in the future. Such was the case with Gibbons's (1990) study of family support and the work of Pithouse and colleagues (Pithouse and Holland 1999; Pithouse and Lindell 1994, 1996; Pithouse, Holland and Davey 2001). Here, they are not trying to be representative, but to examine particular exemplars.

It is, then, important to be aware, when appraising social work research, of *the extent to which any study can be said to be representative*. Is it, for example, representative in strict statistical terms, such as probability sampling (see below), is it representative in some other way (such as typicality of characteristics), or is there little to indicate its typicality? How far, furthermore, does the study take into account the limitations of representativeness when coming to conclusions?

Sampling methods

There is a range of **sampling** methods through which we would seek to create some degree of statistical representativeness. Sampling occurs when we seek to obtain some but not all of a particular population, and try to draw conclusions about that whole population on the basis of the findings of that survey. For example, we might wish to get older people's views about the threat to them of violent crime. Surveying the whole population of over-65s (even in one area) would be prohibitively expensive. So we might choose to survey one in ten, and draw conclusions about the whole population (of older people) from that.

Probability sampling occurs when we are aware of the probability of the survey group being representative of the population as a whole. A basic principle (particularly when randomization is used) is that a sample is representative of its population if all members of its population have an equal chance of being selected for the study. **Non-probability sampling** occurs when we do not or cannot know the likelihood of members of a particular population being included in the survey.

NON-PROBABILITY SAMPLES

Let us first look at non-probability samples. We already have an idea that many of the surveys carried out on social work itself do not involve probability samples. This is because, as Rubin and Babbie (2001) comment, social work research – and this is equally applicable to health research – is often conducted in situations where it is difficult, or frankly not feasible, to select probability samples. It may not, for example, be feasible to select a probablity sample because of financial constraints – it may simply be too expensive, and the researchers may not have sufficient funding. Rubin and Babbie write this generally in relation to an American context, but it is equally true in relation to Britain. This can be the case with health research, but the scope for probability sampling is greater, partly because many areas of health draw on the population of an area as a whole.

A **convenience sample** is one that is selected without using random procedures or a known probability of selection. This could involve reliance on subjects who are easily available. Representativeness, in statistical terms, can be problematic, in that we do not know to what extent the sample reflects the population about which we are trying to comment. Although we could identify characteristics that might make it in some respects typical (see above). Research on students enrolled on particular courses often represents convenience sampling. Suppose we asked them their motivation for entering social work and coming on a social work course. We might find out what those in that course think, but in statistical terms it is practically impossible to anticipate the possible biases that may arise in the sample. This applies as much, of course, to those on health courses.

Purposive samples are selected with a particular purpose in mind. It can be chosen on the basis of particular research aims, or the researcher's judgement or knowledge. For example, if we are trying to develop comprehensive facilities for older people, we might choose to survey the views of key personnel who have knowledge of service development of older people, together with key individuals who are service users.

Quota samples seek to get a quota of particular groups who comprise the target population. We start with a matrix. Suppose we are seeking African Caribbean views of the accessibility of services in the area. We might seek to look for age, gender and education levels as the basis of choosing the sample. In each area we would seek to replicate the proportions in the African Caribbean population as a whole. Thus, if there were 49 per cent males and 51 per cent females, these are the proportions we would choose. However, imposed on this might be age. We might divide them by under-18s, 18–65s, and 65s and above. We would need to divide the sample into those proportions by age group, but also in each age group represent the proportions of the population that were male and female (see Table 5.1).

Table 5.1 Percentage of population by age and sex		
	Male	Female
<18	50	50
18–65	48	52
65+	44	56

In this case, we would try to reflect, as far as possible, the proportions that occur in each 'cell' in the above table (cells being, for example, the proportion of males under 18 or the proportion of females aged 18 to 65).

Snowball samples are also often mentioned in this context, but are generally used in exploratory qualitative research. This occurs when members of a population are difficult to locate (e.g. homeless individuals). Basically, having identified some individuals, you get them to suggest others who might also be approached, or get information that would enable the researcher to locate others.

All these methods, it should be emphasized, would not be representative, except by the greatest stroke of luck. In quota sampling, because we can choose anyone who fits in a cell, we don't know whether that subgroup would be representative. It may be the first one who comes along. With snowball sampling, anyone who is part of the population group in which we are interested could be chosen, so it is highly likely there will be bias (e.g. they may be part of the same network).

PROBABILITY SAMPLES

A basic principle of probability sampling is that a sample will be representative of its population if all members of that population have an equal chance of being selected in the sample.

Probability sampling offers two advantages over non-probability samples:

1. Probability samples, even if not perfectly representative, are typically more representative than other types of sampling because biases are avoided.

2. Probability theory allows us to estimate the sample's accuracy or representativeness. In non-probability sampling the odds are heavily against selecting a sample that near perfectly represents the population of study, and even if it did we would have no way of knowing it.

Random sampling allows us to obtain a survey sample with a very high likelihood that it is representative of the total population. Random sampling involves random selection of subjects for a survey, in which each member of the total population has an equal chance of selection. The notion of equal chance of selection is easily shown through the toss of a coin. Where we toss a coin, on each occasion it is tossed we have an equal chance of it falling to heads or tails. We might get the following for the first four throws: heads, heads, tails, heads (3 heads, 1 tail). However, on the next throw we would still have a 50–50 chance of getting heads or tails (it is not reduced by the previous results). Over a large number of throws, however, we would expect there to be close to a 50–50 split.

We can estimate, from a probability sample (random), what is called the confidence interval. The confidence interval indicates the degree of confidence that we can have that the random sample is indeed representative of the population as a whole. This is usually expressed in terms of the percentage likelihood that the sample is within +/− a certain percentage of the parameters of the total population, i.e. the characteristics of that population (what it is). Thus we would say that there is a 95 per cent probability that the findings we have are +/−5 percentage points of the population parameters. We see the confidence interval most frequently in election sampling, where this +/−5 per cent is used. This is, of course, important where the two major parties are within 5 percentage points of each other. For example, Labour has 44 per cent and the Conservatives 40 per cent – since we cannot be sure that the Conservatives are not actually 1 point ahead of Labour (or 9 points behind them). The principle is equally relevant to random sampling in relation to other issues.

Systematic sampling is an alternative to random sampling. Here, instead of randomly choosing subjects, we choose systematically every *n*th person. For example, if we have a population of 10,000 and we wish to have a 10 per cent sample for the survey, we would choose every tenth person on a list (totalling 1000).

Stratified random sampling is like quota sampling, except that each individual group is itself randomly chosen. Thus, where 10 per cent of the population is African Caribbean, we would have a sample containing 10 per cent African Caribbean. Within this group, our sample would be chosen randomly.

Sampling may be broadly divided into two forms: probability and non-probability. A basic principle of probability sampling is that a sample will be representative of its population if all members of that population have an equal chance of being selected in the sample. Non-probability sampling is unable to achieve the standards required by that principle.

Types of survey

In general the literature identifies three types of survey:

- postal/mail surveys
- telephone surveys
- face-to-face interviews.

Postal/mail surveys

These are surveys sent through the post, filled in by the respondent themselves, and returned by post. They are filled in (where they are) 'cold' by people who usually had no reason to expect it. These surveys generally involve relatively brief questionnaires that are easily completed. They need to be self-explanatory, using clear and simple statements. The upshot of this is that the degree of depth and detail in a postal questionnaire is likely to be quite limited. This, it follows, means that there are limitations to the depth of analysis that can be achieved in the report itself. Biases can also arise through low response rates.

Quite *high response rates* can be achieved where the topic is *highly relevant to the respondent.* For example, if we were to survey GPs about the quality of management in the NHS (particularly tied to service development) we might well get a high response rate. The same would probably not be said if it were sent to the general public, many of whom would be quite bemused by such a questionnaire.

Telephone surveys

Here respondents are selected randomly from a telephone directory. These are widely used, though rather less so in social work.

Most households these days have telephones, so the possibility of bias (to the better off) is reduced compared with the past. However, social workers very frequently work with the poorest, sometimes transient populations, and these are far more likely not to have a telephone. The result is that a telephone survey is likely to exclude the very people that social workers frequently deal with to a greater extent than other population groups. In principle this may be less of a problem in relation to areas of health service provision. For example, health staff in a health centre or general practice work generally with a wide spectrum of the general population (although this may, as with health visiting, tend towards particular age ranges). Nevertheless, even here the most deprived groups may be expected to have telephones with less frequency (or, as I once found in my research, to have had one, but been 'cut off' for non-payment of bills). There is likely to be a bias towards less deprived groups.

The advantages of telephone surveys include the fact that they are cheap and efficient. They can cover a wide geographical area, and do not require a great deal of travelling time and expense. Compared with postal questionnaires, telephone surveys can involve greater depth and detail. However, longer interviews, over 45 minutes, are unlikely to be practicable, particularly so if consultation of records is required (e.g. when they had the last hospital admission).

Face-to-face interviews

Here information is generally collected in the respondent's own home or at some other venue convenient to the respondent. This is the most resource-hungry and expensive survey methods, but it provides the opportunity for the greatest depth and detail of analysis. It also allows more control over the process of information collection (e.g. if the interviewer thinks the respondent is affected by the presence of others in the room they can try to see them separately). Likewise, it is possible to build up a rapport, which enables the interview to be more personalized.

On the other hand the expense and resource-hungry nature of the face-to-face interview means that the sample size is likely to be smaller. Respondents may also be more hesitant about giving personal details when someone is right in front of them. They may feel constrained to give socially acceptable responses (e.g. on racial attitudes). There may be a tendency to over-report socially desirable behaviour.

Presenting data – descriptive statistics

Descriptive statistics is a method of presenting findings from questionnaire-based surveys in a manageable way, and it is characteristic of much health and social work research. A survey of 200 people with 100 questions leads to 20,000 answers, clearly far too much to cope with on a person-by-person basis. Descriptive statistics is concerned primarily with aggregation. It tells us cumulatively what the tendencies are in the data, and can give us an idea of variation in aggregates.

Univariate analysis – Distribution

In the analysis of distribution of cases we can look at one variable at a time (univariate analysis). Take age:

>   38 years – 5 cases
>
>   39 years – 2 cases
>
>   40 years – 6 cases
>
>   41 years – 3 cases
>
>   and so on.

However, a more manageable format is to group data:

18–44 years	40 (20%)
45–64 years	100 (50%)
65+ years	60 (30%)

We have a clearer idea of groupings and range, but less detail – for example, we don't know how many exactly were aged 39.

One problem is **missing data**. At times we do not have full information on respondents. Again we might be missing five cases from 200 in terms of age (but not other factors). We can report the proportion (percentage) including the missing data (i.e. of 200) or excluding it (percentage of 195).

CENTRAL TENDENCY

The central tendency is identified in terms of the mean, median and mode:

- **Mean** is the average for all cases (e.g. the average age might be 45).

- **Median** is the middle attribute on ranked distribution (of 11 cases, this would be the 6th).

- **Mode** is the most frequently occurring attribute (e.g. we may have more people aged 37 than any other single age).

We focus on central tendency like this when it helps presentation and informs. A good example of this is from one of the early stages of my maternal depression and child care research (Sheppard 1997c). In this I had 39 problem areas. I collapsed a detailed 39 variable problem questionnaire into its five main domains (social instrumental, social relationship, health, parenting, and child problems). For example, in the realm of child problems we included cognitive difficulties, social withdrawal, and behavioural difficulties and educational underachievement (amongst others). In each of these five domains I was able to get central tendency scores, which enabled me to identify which were the most prevalent (I had to identify this in terms of weighting domains, because the number of problem areas in each domain varied). The results are shown in Table 5.2.

Table 5.2 Weighted average number of problems identified in problem domains related to depression and severe depression (from Sheppard 1997c)

	Entire population	Not depressed	Depressed (excl. severely depressed)	Severely depressed
Social	2.01	1.82	2.13	2.74
Relationship	2.90	2.82	2.96	3.22
Health	1.21	1.04	0.95	2.48
Parenting	2.52	2.41	2.60	2.89
Child	1.84	1.80	1.85	2.00

This table can be examined in a number of ways. However, to take some examples, we can see that, taking the entire group, relationship problems were experienced to a greater degree than other problems, and that those least experienced were health problems. We can also see that severely depressed mothers experienced more problems in all problem domains than both depressed mothers and mothers who were not depressed at all.

While an average gives a single number with a central tendency, it comes at the cost of **dispersion** of results (i.e. the range of variation). For example, our mean age may be 45, but our range may be 18 to 75 (where 18 is the youngest person in the sample, and 75 is the oldest). Standard deviation is a sophisticated and rather complex measure of dispersion. Interested readers who wish to tackle the topic can read the section at the end of this chapter (p.108).

Bivariate and multivariate analysis

We can look for differences between subgroups within our population. We can take, for example, men's and women's attitudes to child care. We could present the question posed in Table 5.3 to a sample of 400 equally divided between men and women.

Table 5.3 Do men, in general, take sufficient part in looking after their children?

	Men	Women	Total
Yes	120 (60%)	60 (30%)	180 (45%)
No	80 (40%)	140 (70%)	220 (55%)
Total	200	200	400

Now, if we look at overall results we would see that there was some, but not a great, tendency to see men as not contributing enough. However, this hides strong differences, based on sex, between men and women – the former generally thinking men did OK and the latter even more frequently thinking they did not.

This type of table is often called a contingency table, because the dependent variable (attitudes to child care) is contingent on the independent variable (sex of participant).

Multivariate tables are extensions of bivariate tables. Table 5.4 is from one of my research projects looking at maternal depression and child welfare concerns in clients of health visitors and social workers. This table looks at the relationship between maternal depressed status, client status, and concerns about child abuse. I have presented the findings just in percentages, for clarity of understanding. In fact there were 701 clients of health visitors and 116 clients of social workers (mothers, that is). Those mothers actually on social work caseloads were not included in the health visitor data of the following table. Here we have three variables: presence of, or concerns about, child abuse, presence or absence of depression, and client status – social worker or health visitor.

Table 5.4 Rates of depression (expressed as percentages) in clients related to profession and concerns about abuse (from Sheppard 1998b)

	Not depressed	Depressed	Total
Social work – abuse	54	46	100
Social work – no abuse	73	27	100
Health visitor – abuse concerns	69	31	100
Health visitor – no abuse concerns	92	8	100
$p < 0.0001$			

The table shows clearly:

- that the highest rates of depression were manifested in depressed mothers who were social work clients, and the lowest in non-depressed mothers who were health visitor clients
- that in both the abuse and non-abuse categories the rates of depression were higher in the social work group than the corresponding health visitor group

- that nevertheless health visitor families where there were abuse concerns had rates of maternal depression comparable to social work families where there were no abuse concerns.

These are important findings if we are to understand issues relating to community child care professionals, and the responsibilities they carry. They do not, of course, suggest that health visitors somehow 'work less' than social workers. They are, however, consistent with features of the two professions which we know to be the case: that while health visitors tend to work with a group reflective of the general population, social workers have a more marginalized group of clients, who are the subject of intervention precisely because of their high levels of problems and needs.

Question: Are the tables in the research you are using presented in such a way as to make the data understandable and easy to access?

So does the difference make any difference?

The null hypothesis

How can we be sure that differences between two groups represent real and important differences between them? If we find that group A (say working-class women) have rates of depression of 20 per cent, and group B (say middle-class women) have rates of depression of only 10 per cent, is this difference actually significant? What about if the rates are 20 per cent working-class women and 15 per cent middle-class women? Or 20 per cent working-class and 18 per cent middle-class women?

The alternative (or at least one alternative) is that these results are a matter of chance – of pot luck. Just like in dealing a pack of cards you might be dealt a series of cards of the same suit (even though there are four suits) so differences between two groups can be a matter of chance.

How do we deal with this? Statistical significance tests are designed to indicate the likelihood of the null hypothesis being the case. The null hypothesis is the hypothesis that differences are a matter of chance. So we might have:

(a) *Main hypothesis:* Working-class women will experience higher rates of depression than middle-class women.

(b) *Null hypothesis:* Differences between working- and middle-class women are a matter of chance.

The scale through which significance, or probability (p), is measured is 0 to 1. Where the significance test yields a result of $p = 1$, this means the results may be considered totally a matter of chance (i.e. that the null hypothesis is correct). But the smaller the figure, the less likely the results are a matter of chance. Thus:

$p = 0.1$ means there is a 10 per cent probability that results are a matter of chance

$p = 0.05$ means there is a 5 per cent probability that results are a matter of chance

$p = 0.01$ means there is a 1 per cent probability that results are a matter of chance (i.e. there is a 99 per cent likelihood that the results represent real differences between the two groups).

Significance tests are given in terms of decimals, so we are likely to see results involving figures like 0.1 (1 in 10), 0.05 (1 in 20) or 0.01 (one in a hundred) etc.

Statistical significance

But where do we draw the line? Should we consider a test score of 0.5 has a high probability of representing a real difference between the groups, rather than a matter of chance? What about 0.1? Or 0.05?

Take a result of 0.75. This would mean that there was a 75 per cent probability that differences were a matter of chance. Clearly, it is highly likely that results were simply a matter of pot luck. What about 0.5? This represents a 50:50 likelihood that results represented chance. Again far from a convincing case. That is the point. At what point can we consider the data present a convincing case that results are not down to chance?

Any cut-off point is going to be arbitrary. If we put a cut-off point at 0.1, does this mean that a result of 0.11 is not significant, but one of 0.099 is? Well, yes actually! The important thing is that we set, in advance, the level at which we can consider the results to be significant, and there are certain conventions.

Most put the 'cut-off' point as 0.05. That is there is a 1 in 20 probability that results are a matter of chance, and 19 in 20 that they are not. Key levels of significance are usually expressed as:

> $p < 0.05$: less than 1 in 20 probability that results are a matter of chance

> $p < 0.01$: less than 1 in 100 probability that results are a matter of chance

> $p < 0.001$: less than 1 in 1000 probability that results are a matter of chance

> $p < 0.0001$: less than 1 in 10,000 probability that the results are a matter of chance

Two-tailed tests

Statisticians commonly make a distinction between one- and two-tailed tests. This is about the direction of the association. Did A cause B or did B cause A?

Suppose we were to find poor maternal attachment (towards children) and maternal depression were associated. For example, take the hypothesis:

> (a) Mothers who are depressed (b) display poorer attachment towards their young children.

Here we have one direction of association: depression to poor child attachment. This is a directional hypothesis. However, suppose there was a possibility that poor child attachment led (say through poor parenting performance, making the woman feel low self-esteem) to depression? That would be completely the opposite direction. This, by the way, is entirely plausible. It provides an opposite direction for association.

- Tests that test only one direction of association (a directional hypothesis) are called **one-tailed tests**.

- Tests that cover *both* possible directions (a non-directional hypothesis) are called **two-tailed tests**.

Where we can realistically see two alternative possibilities, then we should use a two-tailed test, which, by the way, is more difficult to 'pass'!

If we look again at Table 5.4, we find a *p* value of <0.0001. The test undertaken (a 'chi- squared test', which need not detain us) used a two-tailed approach. Hence using the more stringent approach, the likelihood that these results were a matter of chance was less than one in ten thousand. This, of course, should give us a very high degree of confidence indeed that the findings reflected some underlying trend.

Where two or more groups are being compared, it is possible to assess the significance of these differences, through statistical tests, the results of which can be clearly apparent to the reader from simple presentation (e.g. see Table 5.4).

Conclusion

It is quite apparent that there are many aspects to surveys and sampling. These include quite technical elements. Nevertheless, the fundamentals of both processes make considerable intuitive sense. Sampling provides us with a way of looking at features such as tendencies in particular groups (or populations), and how these differ from other groups (or populations). What however do we do when we want to look at interventions (say counselling by district nurses and health visitors)? How are we to evaluate the outcomes of these interventions? One way of doing this is to conduct and experiment, and it is to this that we turn in the next chapter.

Note: Calculating standard deviation

We need to consider standard deviation (SD) in terms of a normal distribution. A normal distribution tends to produce the greatest number of cases around the average producing what is called a bell-shaped curve.

When we can assume that our data have a normal distribution, then approximately 34 per cent will fall within one standard deviation of the mean (i.e. 34% above and 34% below, i.e. 68%).

Now the standard deviation can be calculated, and it will not be the same for each study. We might, though, be looking at health or social work caseloads, and have 10 practitioners in the team with an average caseload of 30. Where the standard deviation happens to be 2, we would know that just over 2/3 of social workers had caseloads between 28 and 32.

With ordinal measures (where we do not know the distance between scores, e.g. where a range of very satisfied to very dissatisfied is 5 points), it is inappropriate to give a standard deviation score.

So how is it done?

Table 5.5 Calculating standard deviation

Caseload	Mean	Caseload minus mean	Deviation squared
28	30	−2	4
34	30	4	16
31	30	1	1
29	30	−1	1

1. Calculate the mean.

2. Subtract the mean from each value in our sample.

3. Square each deviation.

4. Divide sum of the squares by number of cases in our study (say 10).

5. Then obtain the square root of the result (i.e. square root of 40/10 = square root of 4 = 2).

Hence SD is 2, and 68 per cent will be within +/−2 of average.

Exercises

5.1 Some issues that can be discussed after reading this chapter

- What is a survey?
- What are the key issues in considering sample representativeness?
- What is non-probabilistic sampling? Consider the different types and characteristics of this sampling.
- What are the strengths and weaknesses of different types of survey?
- What is the difference between bivariate and univariate analysis? Comment on some of the issues to consider when examining tables.

5.2 An exercise in appraising and using research

Consider one of the following papers (or another of your choice – see list on the following page) that use a survey method:

Shor, R. (2000) 'Child maltreatment: Differences in perceptions between parents in low and middle income neighbourhoods.' *British Journal of Social Work 30*, 2, 165–179.

Margolius, F. and Hudson, K. (1995) 'Beliefs and perceptions about children in pain: A survey.' *Pediatric Nursing 21*, 2, 111–115.

Consider this paper in the light of a critical analysis of surveys as a methodology/way of getting understanding:

- Outline the background to the study and problem formulation.

- Why did the author consider the survey the best way to obtain the information they sought?

- How far did the author seek to gain representativeness in the sample of the target population (e.g. typicality, randomization, etc.)? What kind of sample did they develop? What was their sampling frame?

- What are the findings of the study? Are there any gaps in information?

- What are the conclusions? Are the conclusions justified by the evidence presented? Does the author identify the limits to the study?

- How useful is this study for practice?

Examples of research employing survey approaches

Abbney, A., Schneider, J. and Mozley, C. (1999) 'Visitors' views on residential homes.' *British Journal of Social Work 29*, 567–579.

Doel, M. and Sawdon, C. (2001) 'What makes for successful groupwork? A survey of agencies in the UK.' *British Journal of Social Work 31*, 337–363.

Hatfield, B., Mohammad, H., Rahim, Z. and Tanweer, H. (1996) 'Mental health and the Asian communities: A local survey.' *British Journal of Social Work 26*, 315–337.

Kahn, R. *et al.* (2000)' State income inequality, household income and maternal mental health: A cross sectional national survey.' *British Medical Journal 321*, 1311–1315.

Marino, B. and Marino, E. (2000) 'Parents' report of children's hospital care: What it means for your practice.' *Pediatric Nursing 26*, 2, 195–198.

Reifler, B. and Cohen, W. (1998) 'Practice of geriatric psychiatry and mental health services for the elderly: Results of an international study.' *International Psychogeriatrics 10*, 4, 351–357.

Scholle, E., Colton, M., Casas, F. *et al.* (1999) 'Perceptions of stigma and user involvement in child welfare services.' *British Journal of Social Work 29*, 373–379.

Sheppard, M. (1999) 'Social profile, maternal depression and welfare concerns in clients of health visitors and social workers: A comparative study.' *Children and Society 12*, 125–135.

Further reading

Aldridge, A. and Levine, K. (2001) *Surveying the Social World*. Buckingham: Open University Press.

Bryman, A. (1995) *Quality and Quantity in Social Research*. London: Unwin Hyman.

de Vaus, D. (1992) *Surveys in Social Research*. London: UCL Press.

Hammersley, M. and Atkinson, P. (1995) *Ethnography: Principles in Practice*. London: Routledge. (Chapter 1 – contains criticism.)

Moser, C. and Kalton, G. (1997) *Survey Methods in Social Investigation*. London: Heinemann.

Sapsford, R. (1999) *Survey Research*. London: Sage.

CHAPTER SIX

Experimental and Quasi-Experimental Designs

When we practise, how do we know that what we are doing is doing any good? This would seem to be the question of greatest importance in health and social work – for practitioners at any rate.

Suppose you were a health visitor, and you felt that counselling may be particularly helpful for women who had been through emergency Caesareans when they gave birth. You may reason that these women had expected to give birth in the 'conventional' way, that there had been (in all likelihood) some kind of foetal distress, that this was likely to have been a worry to the woman. This may have been followed by a general anaesthetic, and a birth at which the woman was not conscious. She will come round, having had surgery, and with a baby introduced to her for the first time. For anyone who knows anything about counselling, this description carries a whole load of areas of psychological threat and potential distress. The sense of 'loss' that she was unable to see the birth, of failure to give birth in the conventional way, of intrusion as a result of the surgery, and of powerlessness at being unconscious for one of the most important events of her life. In addition the mother is impaired at the point of birth, by the disability brought on by the operation. She is unable to respond as positively as she would like, and be a 'mother', in the sense she may have hoped. Indeed, she may well have a general sense of failure as a mother.

As a health visitor you may wish to combat this psychological distress, and help the mother, for her own sake, to come to terms with the Caesarean birth. Indeed, the impact could be such that there is a longer-term impairment of her capacity to parent, because of the effect on her confidence and self-esteem. Counselling may well appear an efficacious response to these circumstances.

Let us look at the social worker. You may come across a family circumstance where there is a parent with mild learning difficulties who is nevertheless having difficulties with their eight-year-old boy. There has been difficulty setting boundaries, and the child is increasingly refusing to respond to quite reasonable requests, such as coming to tea at the right time, or limiting their television watching, and is becoming defiant and aggressive.

You may wish to help the mother set up a step-by-step regime, in which their capacity to have consistent expectations and the child's capacity to respond to them are improved to the point where the family is functioning satisfactorily. This might point to a task-centred approach, with its incremental strategy focused on the creation of positive behaviours, and its capacity to help people learn effective strategies for problem solving.

In the two cases mentioned, one involving the health visitor and the other involving the social worker, there are very good reasons to consider undertaking intervention, indeed the intervention suggested. But how do we know whether such intervention would work? How far might counselling make a difference to the mother's emotional state, or her capacity to parent? To what extent are relations, and child behaviour, improved by the use of task-centred practice? These are issues of intervention effectiveness, and it is one to which a considerable effort has been put by social researchers. One way, then, of identifying the right kind of intervention is to find out whether it has been shown to be effective. This requires us to look at the relevant research.

The issue of effectiveness is one to which we will turn again and again, but it is the very strong belief by its advocates that experimental designs represent the best means for evaluating effectiveness. What do we mean by effectiveness? And what kinds of ways can we evaluate effectiveness?

Effectiveness involves effectiveness in achieving some goal or outcome. Thus we would be concerned, with child abuse for example, with social workers' capacity to ensure parenting improved to the point where abuse no longer occurred. Or with young offenders, we might be concerned about reducing the likelihood of young offenders continuing their offending behaviour. Our goals would be to prevent recurrence of abuse or offending behaviour in the individual instance, and to reduce the rate of child abuse occurrence or offending in terms of the population with which they work. Or with young mothers with difficulties in maternal involvement with a child, our goal, as health visitors, could be to increase interaction through play.

To understand effectiveness we need to look at change. Why is this the case? Well, in the case of social work, we are generally dealing with people with problems, which, for our purposes, means that, at the very least, social workers are trying to prevent any further deterioration in circumstances or condition, or, more desirably, they are seeking to get some improvement. The same is frequently the case with health workers, only in relation to illness (although many health workers might cite 'maintaining health' to be their primary focus). We may wish to improve the mobility of an older person, or the social integration of someone suffering a mental illness, or reduce the amount and severity of tantrums in a young child.

What this means is that we have to measure things over a period of time. That is because the idea of change or maintenance implies a period over which either of these would have occurred.

At the heart of evaluation is the achievement of some desired outcome, and for this to have occurred over some time period.

These are the basics. How do they look in relation to experimental designs?

Experimental designs

At the heart of experimental designs are two groups:

- the *experimental (E) group*, which receives the intervention or programme to be evaluated
- the *control (C) group*, which does not receive the intervention or programme.

So, the essence of experimental designs is a contrast between haves (E group) and have-nots (C group). When we carry out an experiment we allocate some people to the experimental group and others to the control group. The experiment, therefore, is a comparison between the two groups.

Two other key concepts relate to variables. Variables refer to particular and important factors in a situation. For example, one variable might be offending behaviour, or presence of clinical depression. These might be considered as problems. Other variables can relate to particular intervention elements, for example the use of family support workers.

The **dependent variable** is the variable that is acted upon. It is generally the issue or problem about which we are concerned. So, if we are concerned with dealing with the problem of depression, then the existence or severity of depression would be the dependent variable.

The **independent variable** is the variable which is doing the acting. It is the variable that, we hope, will be shown to cause the change. So, if we felt that a particular form of intervention, say the provision of a family support worker to help with child care and home management for the depressed mother, was going to be the agent of change, this would be the independent variable.

There is a further key issue, that of the **hypothesis**, which brings together the dependent and independent variables. The hypothesis is a statement of an outcome that the researcher is proposing will occur. For example, a hypothesis could be:

> The use of family support workers, providing support for mothers, will have the outcome of reducing rates of depression.

The experimental (E) group is characterized by being in receipt of the independent variable (e.g. the family support worker). The control (C) group is characterized by not being in receipt of the independent variable. We then seek to compare the outcomes for the two groups.

If we find that improvement in the E group is significantly greater than in the C group, we will conclude that the independent variable is indeed effective. Thus, were this to occur with family support workers and depression, we would conclude that the use of family support workers is effective in reducing depression.

So much for the bare bones. However, there are a number of significant technical issues that must be observed for research to be considered an experiment.

Quasi-experimental designs

Quasi-experimental designs provide an alternative to experimental designs where fulfilling the criteria of experimental designs is not possible. Like experimental designs, quasi-experimental designs involve two groups: an experimental group, upon which the intervention takes place, and a comparison group, upon which it does not. It involves an independent variable (the particular intervention being evaluated) and dependent variable (that which is supposed to be affected). It also involves measurement of change over time with baseline and follow-up measures. The difference lies in the inability to assign subjects randomly to experimental and control group.

The most frequently identified are **non-equivalent control groups**. This is where the two groups cannot be randomly assigned from a common pool. In these circumstances we seek an alternative way of obtaining a comparison group that appears similar to the experimental group. We can do this by finding two comparable environments, one subject to the innovative experiment and another which does not. The kinds of factors (which do depend on the focus of the study) that would be relevant are age, socio-economic status, mental status, ethnicity, and social functioning.

Say we were interested in the impact of the use of reminiscence therapy on the morale and psychological well-being of older people residents of nursing homes. We might look at two nursing homes, one where the reminiscence therapy occurred and the other where it did not. We would seek to make sure that the two groups were similar in all significant respects. We would also wish to establish that they were equivalent in the dependent variables – morale and psychological well-being. If the average scores in the dependent variable were similar, it would be reasonable to assume that differences at follow-up would represent the effects of the intervention.

If we found that improvements in the experimental group were greater than in the comparison group we would have reasonable grounds to believe that the effect was caused by reminiscence work. It may be that the change represented some continuous up–down fluctuation in morale and well-being, or even a freak occurrence. However, we could establish through multiple observation, before and after the experimental intervention, whether this really did represent a change.

Quasi-experimental designs differ from experimental design in that there is not complete equivalence of experimental and control groups.

Key technical elements

Comparability

RANDOMIZATION

The two groups, to be comparable, must be similar. It is no good finding there are big differences in outcome for the E group compared with the C group if the two groups are very different. If they are very different (say in number of children, income or available supporters) then it could be these, rather than the independent variable (the family support worker) that reduces levels of depression. The best means for achieving this is a process of randomization (hence they are called randomized controlled trials).

There is no way we can guarantee the E and C groups will be equivalent in all respects. Randomization, though, does provide a way to guarantee a high mathematical likelihood that the differences will be insignificant. Randomization is the random assignment of individuals to the E and C groups. The subjects randomly assigned will be from a population. So with our depression/family support worker example we would, say, have a population of community psychiatric nurse or health visitor clients or child and family care social service users.

Random allocation involves the use of probability sampling techniques. The simplest form (often used in experiments) is the toss of a coin. Thus we might allocate all individuals for whom a head was thrown to the E group, and all those with tails to the C group. As a general rule, the larger the sample the better. Thus, obviously, if we have only two, there is no particular reason to assume each is similar to the other. Where we have 100 or 1000 there will be an ever-increasing likelihood of similarity.

MATCHING

Comparability can sometimes be better achieved by matching. Matching can be done without randomization. What we would seek to do with matching is to make sure each group is comparable in terms of certain key characteristics. Thus we might seek to achieve comparability by, for example, age, number of children and race. We would seek to reflect the proportions of these in the population in both groups. Thus if 40 per cent of mothers were aged under 30 and 60 per cent were 30 or over, this would be reflected in the groups. If 60 per cent of women had one or two children and 40 per cent had three or more, this too would be reflected. And so on.

A true experiment involves random allocation within these sub-groups. Thus, having identified the 40 per cent of mothers aged under 30, we would then randomly allocate them to the E and C groups through the toss of a coin. Likewise for the 60 per cent aged 30 and over.

Table 6.1 Random allocation involving subgroups		
	Women < 30	Women 30+
1 or 2 children	16	24
3+ children	24	36
Total	40	60

We would here randomly allocate each of these groups one at a time. The 16 women under the age of 30 with one or two children would be randomly allocated, then the next of the three groups one at a time.

The desired result, whether in randomization or matching, is that the E group should be the same as the C group (or so similar as not to matter). When considering assignment of subjects to E and C groups we should be aware of two points:

1. We may not know in advance what the relevant variables are for the matching process.

2. Most of the statistics used to evaluate experiments assume randomization. Failure to design experiments that way makes later use of these statistics less meaningful.

Independent variables and change

These are two other key distinguishing elements of the experiment. We introduce the independent variable (family support worker) to the experimental group, while withholding it from the control group. We then seek to measure the amount of **change** over a period of time speci-

fied in advance of the experiment. We might, for example, look at matters at the end of six months. Alternatively we may do so after a year or
longer. Or we could make multiple measurements (six months, 12
months, 18 months).

Change involves the notions of baseline and follow-up measures.
Baseline measures are made at the beginning point of the experiment.
These measure the dependent variables at the beginning. So we might
want to take a measurement of severity of depression at the outset. At the
follow-up we would look at the same variable (measure of depression).
We would seek to see if it was the same, worse or better.

If we were looking at effectiveness regarding depression, we would
hypothesize that significantly more women in the E group would not be
depressed at follow-up than those in the control group. Of course,
strictly speaking, we don't know that any improvement will hold for
periods other than those measured. For example we don't know that
two years later the E group will have maintained their improvement lead
over the C group. However, with practice, where we seek to be knowl-
edge-based, we are always looking at the balance of evidence or, indeed,
where any evidence exists.

In order that we can measure change, we need to have **standardization** in the instruments we are using. By this I mean that there needs to
be known consistency in the ways that the instruments are used to carry
out their measurements. If, for example, an instrument is to be of any
value in measuring depression, then it is no good if:

- in identical situations it gives different measures, or
- in different situations it gives the same or similar measures.

We could not be sure, for example, that any measured change actually
reflected some real change in the subject's circumstances or, conversely,
that a measurement of no change reflected that nothing had altered in
relation to outcome measures. The way this is achieved is, generally, by
the use of instruments with known reliability and validity (such as the

Edinburgh Scale or the Beck Depression Inven

some confidence that there is consistency of meas

> Experiments consist of two groups. One group (t
> group) receives the 'input' that we wish to evaluate; t
> (the control group) does not. We are able to measure t
> the input by measuring and comparing the degree of ...ge over
> time in the experimental and control groups.

Causation

Those who conduct experiments are seeking to establish that the independent variable is the cause of changes in the dependent variable(s). We
need to understand the logic of causal inference. Under what circumstances can we infer that changes in the dependent variable were caused
by the independent variable, rather than some other factor or factors?
We always need to consider whether there are any possible rival explanations, and whether these can be ruled out. There are generally considered to be three criteria for inferring causality:

- time order
- empirical correlation
- no other factors.

The first requirement of a causal relationship between two variables is
that the cause precedes the effect in time (i.e. the independent variable
should come before the dependent variable). It makes no sense to argue
that something is caused by something else that happened after the
change took place. This is not as straightforward as it appears. For example we know there is a relationship between relapse in schizophrenia
and high expressed emotion (EE) by relatives (the core of which is hostility). We can establish high EE is the cause of relapse. However, it is
more difficult to establish whether high EE is the cause of the onset of
schizophrenia in the first place. It may be that it is indeed the cause.
Alternatively, the opposite may be the case: the odd behaviour of the

...phrenic person may be responsible for an ever-growing irritation ...n the part of relatives, which leads to outright hostility (Kuipers, Leff and Lam 2002; Leff and Vaughn 1985).

Another feature which can complicate matters is that individuals may anticipate something happening. Where, for example, a woman's sister emigrates to Australia, it may be that she grieves about this, and may even become depressed following the departure. However, it is possible for the grieving to begin before the departure. In this case the woman would be anticipating the loss of her sister, and experiencing anticipatory grief.

The point is, humans are not inanimate objects. They think, understand, anticipate, and act. They therefore can take actions that can impact on the causal sequence of events. People sometimes change their behaviour in anticipation of some event. Advocates of experiments consider that anticipatory acts should be given some consideration when we deal with the issue of causality.

The second requirement of a causal relationship is that the two variables should be empirically correlated with each other. It would make no sense to say that the loss of a loved one causes depression if we find, in a population that suffers grief, there is no correlation with depression. However, things are still not that simple.

We are not likely to find that there is a perfect correlation between the independent variable and dependent variable. Take, for example, my research on depressed mothers. Here we find a significant association between the presence of depression in mothers and child abuse (Sheppard 1997b). But, it is not a perfect relationship. There are many cases where mothers were depressed but their children had *not* been abused. Likewise, there were cases where mothers were not depressed and their children had been abused.

We need to remember the essentially probabilistic nature of the social world. This case suggests, as with other research, that other factors played a part. Maybe some depressed mothers got support from elsewhere, and hence no abuse occurred despite the presence of depression. Likewise, other factors such as economic stress may play a part.

The third requirement is that the observed correlation between two variables cannot be explained away as the result of some other factor, not accounted for in the experiment, that may have a causal relationship with both identified variables. In my research, for instance, the depression and the abuse might be associated with other causal factors. Another, well-documented, relationship is that between depression and the presence of social support – here there is an inverse relationship. High rates of depression are associated with low levels of social support. Does that mean that a low level of social support causes depression (or, indeed, that the reverse is the case)? Well, not necessarily. There may be a third factor, perhaps involving personality, that makes the person both more likely to be depressed and also a poorer social mixer.

> Causation involves three elements. The first requirement of a causal relationship between two variables is that the cause precedes the effect in time – the independent variable should come before the dependent variable. The second requirement of a causal relationship is that the two variables should be empirically correlated with each other. The third requirement is that the observed correlation between two variables cannot be explained away as the result of some other factor, not accounted for in the experiment, that may have a causal relationship with the identified variables.

Threats to validity

There are many technical issues that can threaten the certainty with which we can attribute changes in the dependent variable occurring because of the independent variable.

We must first come to terms with some terms! **Internal validity** refers to the confidence we have that the results of a study accurately depict whether one variable is, or is not, the cause of another. To the extent that the three criteria we have outlined are met (cause preceding effect, correlation, and some other factor not responsible) a study will have internal validity. To the extent that we do not meet these criteria, we are not able to claim the independent variable caused the change in the dependent variable. **External validity** refers to the extent to which the causal relationship presented in the study can be generalized beyond the study context and setting.

What kinds of threat can occur to internal validity? The classical exposition of this can be found in Campbell and Stanley's (1963) *Experimental and Quasi Experimental Designs for Research.*

Some factors that can affect matters:

- selection bias
- maturation/passage of time
- lack of precision in measurement
- drop-outs and sample attrition
- intervention fidelity
- infection/diffusion/contamination of groups
- resistance to case assignment protocols
- client recruitment and retention.

SELECTION BIAS

It is clear that experimental and quasi-experimental designs seek to go to great lengths to prevent selection bias. Comparison cannot have any meaning unless the comparison groups are comparable. Suppose, however, we allocated participants to groups on the basis of voluntary participation. We would not be able to attribute any improvement to intervention because other differences between the groups might explain the differences.

Suppose we were examining some group therapy with people with alcohol dependence syndrome. If we allocated to groups on the basis of voluntary participation, the two groups could be quite different. Those not participating might generally be less motivated to change than those who did participate. Not volunteering becomes a way by which subjects actually avoid trying to confront the difficult decisions involved in seeking to change. Those participating in the group, therefore, would have been motivated more than programme refusers – they may have been trying harder, and doing any number of things not directly involved in the intervention that may have affected matters.

Properly conducted experimental and quasi-experimental designs attempt specifically to deal with selection bias by creating comparable groups. *Appraisal of experimental designs, however, should look at the possibility of selection bias.*

MATURATION/PASSAGE OF TIME

Another factor that needs to be guarded against, and is guarded against in properly designed experiments, is maturation. People develop and change regardless of whether they are involved in any research. This change can be in a positive direction, so improvements identified over time can be the result of just that: changes occurring over the passage of time.

One example of this from Rubin and Babbie (2001) is of a counselling programme for victims of rape. If we merely rated the mood state and social functioning of the victims before and after intervention, we might well find improvements (say over a six-month or one-year period). However, this could be the result of the passage of time – a reduction of feelings of trauma as the event became more distant. The same might be said of bereavement counselling. This shows the problem of having a baseline follow-up design with only one group, and without a control group. Without an equivalent group we have a potential rival hypothesis that maturation is responsible for change.

LACK OF PRECISION IN MEASUREMENT

Where we do not have precision and consistency in measurement of dependent or independent variables, we cannot be sure, when measuring change, that change has taken place. For example, if we do not have reliable instruments, then any change that takes place over time may simply reflect inconsistent measures at follow-up compared with the baseline measure. Change is merely the result of instrument inconsistency rather than a real change in situation.

Sometimes the independent variable may not be defined clearly. There are studies where social casework, or social work, is the independent variable, as with Corney's (1984) study of the effectiveness of social work in general medical practice in relation to female depression. While it may be possible to provide a general definition of social work or social casework, the ways in which it operates in the actual circumstances of working with a client may be quite variable. Indeed, what each social worker understands by social casework may differ quite markedly, likewise their capacity actually to carry this out. As with anything, there is liable to be considerable difference in skill levels. This is not like evaluating penicillin in relation to tonsillitis. We know that each pill is exactly the same. This cannot be said about some social interventions. *We need, therefore, to have the most tightly defined intervention possible, with, where relevant, properly trained individuals. This is something else on which we should focus when appraising a study.*

DROP-OUTS AND SAMPLE ATTRITION

Drop-outs and sample attrition present another threat to the integrity of experimental designs, one which is less resolvable by the use of specific techniques – as is the case with randomization in relation to selection bias. Most studies have subjects who drop out in the course of conducting the experiment. Having taken considerable care to make sure both experimental and control groups are comparable, the attrition of the E group means that they would no longer be comparable in the same way. *We need, therefore, to pay attention to the degree of attrition that takes place, since where it becomes too great this would jeopardize the integrity of the study.* The less similar the groups, the less comparable they are.

Suppose we focused on a parenting skills group. Some subjects may drop out, and their reason may be that they see no improvement occurring as a result of the intervention. The drop-outs would systematically bias the results because those who remained would be more likely to have experienced some improvement as a result of the intervention. If we then found that the intervention did indeed lead to improvements greater than those experienced by the control group, this could be mostly to do with losing those in the experimental group for whom it had not proved successful.

INTERVENTION FIDELITY

This refers to the extent to which intervention was delivered as intended. Some areas of social work practice cannot be spelled out in step-by-step manuals. Any lack of clarity in what is involved or potential for doing things in a variety of ways means that different subjects are likely to receive different kinds of service.

There may be some misunderstanding or misinterpretation of what is involved or of the intentions and goals of an intervention or programme. The use of insufficiently trained or unskilled staff can also mean that delivery of the intervention/programme is not consistent, thus compromising the study. There can be staff turnover or organizational changes that may make attending properly to the research protocol (the way it should be carried out) more difficult.

Inevitably, this also has an effect on the extent to which the findings can be *generalized* (external validity). How can we generalize to other circumstances and settings when we cannot be entirely clear about what it is that is being delivered in the first place?

INFECTION/DIFFUSION/CONTAMINATION OF GROUPS

It is quite possible that the E and C groups may be infected by each other. For example, where we are randomly allocating individuals to two groups, the same health or social workers may be conducting the experimental intervention and also working with the control group.

This is perhaps, though, less likely than that they are part of the same organization as other workers who are working with the control group. It may be that awareness of the experimental intervention can affect the way C group workers operate. For example, it may be that health visitors carry out a counselling service for young mothers with child problems. This approach could be adopted by workers with the C group. Likewise, if we are carrying out task-centred work with young offenders, it may be that some, or many, aspects of task-centred work become adopted by C group practitioners who learn of this approach.

There can be contamination in relation to the participants, where they have some contact with each other. This may even extend to occupation of a waiting room, where members of E and C groups may run into each other and inform each other of different strategies for working with problems. This becomes a greater problem where there is more extensive social contact between E and C group members.

RESISTANCE TO CASE ASSIGNMENT PROTOCOLS

Practitioners may actually subvert the process of research because they have different priorities. Rather than a concern with evaluating an intervention, they may be more concerned with responding to need.

Take, for example, a programme that involves intensive social work intervention. The researcher may wish to establish the effectiveness of this particular intervention by allocating participants randomly to experimental and control groups. However, the practitioners may be more concerned with the needs of the individuals concerned, and may seek to allocate those with the most severe problems to the better-resourced intensive intervention. Where they have the opportunity to do this, this can subvert the research design by systematically making the E group a higher-need group, and undermining the comparability of the E and C groups. This problem particularly arises with allocation to an innovative programme.

CLIENT RECRUITMENT AND RETENTION

We have already identified how drop-outs can affect the integrity of an experiment. Clients, furthermore, may resent the use of randomization procedures to determine which service they receive and they may therefore refuse to participate.

> There is a range of factors relating to internal and external validity that are significant in relation to the quality of the research and the confidence that may be attributed to the findings.

Beyond technical issues: Critiques of experimental and quasi-experimental research

Because randomized controlled trials (RCTs) are, according to their advocates, able to deal with a whole series of threats to the integrity of identifying the true cause of any outcome, some have claimed that they provide the soundest foundation on which to base our understanding of what works best.

While there are a number of technical issues to which attention should be given when appraising any experimental design, there are more fundamental issues that some believe undermine the claims made by advocates of RCTs for it being the 'best' form of knowledge.

Causation

There is, some claim, an underlying determinism in experimental designs. This is evident, as we have seen, in the emphasis on looking for a cause for particular outcomes. Thus, when we evaluate a particular intervention, we seek to establish whether this caused some good outcome (e.g. some counselling for grief). When social or health work works, therefore, it does so through a cause–effect relationship between procedures and results of intervention.

However, there is now a strong body of evidence suggesting that an exclusively causal account of human actions is inadequate, except where behaviour is involuntary (e.g. mental illness, compulsive behaviour). Explaining the rest of our behaviour requires some reference to the intentions of people we are studying (i.e. what they wanted to do, and why they wanted to do it). Humans are not inanimate objects – we can't say something caused humans to act in some way, in the way that we can say a fire lit under a pot of water will cause it to attain the temperature of 100 degrees (eventually). People make judgements and decisions of their own, and this is a crucial aspect of understanding human actions.

Take offending behaviour. This has consequences for those who wish to develop causally effective interventions for young offenders. It is necessary to consider their reasons for choosing a course of action (note the word 'choosing' here). This is not to say that choices are not influenced (e.g. by pressures in the social environment, which may be partly predictable in their effects). They cannot, however, be seen as entirely predictable. If people stop offending, it is, in the last analysis, because they choose not to do so, not because they are made to do so by some 'cause'.

Facts – a spurious objectivity?

There is an assumption that evaluation takes place by reference to certain 'facts' about the situation of the subjects studied. Thus, where we might seek to establish that some intervention (e.g. parenting training) led to a reduction in parenting problems or in child abuse, we would, implicitly, be measuring matters against the 'facts' of parenting problems or child abuse.

However, many would suggest that social situations and their definitions are not straightforward, and hence not a simple matter of 'facts'. Take child abuse. This, some (not all, by the way) would argue, is merely a social construction. It is a label put on certain forms of behaviour, in a certain culture, at a certain point in history. What is today regarded as abuse in British (or generally advanced industrial) society might be regarded as good parenting in Victorian times ('spare the rod and spoil the child'), and vice versa. Likewise, female circumcision is desirable in West African culture, but regarded as genital mutilation in dominant British culture. Furthermore, even individual situations involve personal judgements (and hence constructions). What you regard as a parenting problem, as a health or social worker, might not be regarded as such by me (as the parent).

How can you evaluate outcomes when the very stuff of your assessment is contested?

Goals, ends and politics

This is closely related to a concern over the goals of intervention. These are treated as unproblematic in experimental designs (i.e. that it is good to be effective in pursuing the goals outlined in the experiment). The goals are often about the resolution of certain kinds of problems, which some would regard as a social construction, the desirability of which is contested. This is about defining a problem independent of the views of the people experiencing it.

The goals of physicians and their patients may generally be agreed and considered desirable. However, social workers and their clients often disagree about what their problems are (or indeed if they exist). Even where legislation lays down certain responsibilities (e.g. to act to protect children in cases of significant harm), there may be dispute about whether this really exists.

The very goals of health and social work may be politicized. Take young offending. What if some view, as they do, at least part of the reason for offending behaviour in young people to be structural disadvantage? To evaluate the effectiveness of interventions with individuals is to ignore the structural causes of offending behaviour. Likewise, the value that it is important to deal with this offending behaviour may itself be disputed by the offender. Where offending arises in the context of an unequal society, seeking to manage offending behaviour on an individual level might be regarded as oppression of 'have-nots'. The same might be said about inequalities in health. Is it valid to focus primarily on the effectiveness of health remedies in relation to individuals, where social disadvantage plays such a considerable role in an individual's health?

Values, in other words, cannot be taken out of experiments, which are not a matter of dealing with facts alone.

Context, social complexity and extraneous factors

Extraneous factors are considered by advocates of RCTs as a threat to their integrity. For example, if changes beyond the control of researchers are made to the work undertaken with subjects in the research, then this could be a reason for any change achieved, rather than the independent variable.

However, a more profound criticism of the whole process involves the isolation of experiments from the context in which they occur. First, the social world is what philosophers call an 'open system'. By that it is meant that no matter what you seek to do to insulate experiments from some outside factors that can impact on the participants, it is impossible to do so. They are open to all sorts of influences and changes in their lives, any of which may have an impact on the outcome. People do not just 'live in the experiment'. They spend most of their time doing other things, and the experiment is, in terms of time at least, always a very small aspect of their lives. So the desire to prevent outside factors must always fail because human life is simply not like that.

The other point is that any experiment always occurs within its own social context. This is a source of unpredictability. Understanding the contexts that are needed for the mechanisms for change to work is essential for understanding how outcomes are achieved. All kinds of facets may be specific to particular situations: there may be particular local circumstances, culture and expectations. In other words, we can only judge a programme in the context in which it is operating. Feminist methods of intervention with, say, child care problems, or psychological

well-being, will be unlikely to be successful where there ⌐
ditional sex-role stereotype culture operating.

Furthermore, the actual process of conducting experii
seeks to construct it out of reality. People simply do not ɛ
where there is only one variable in operation (the independᴇᴎɪ variable).
They exist in worlds where any number of elements are all interacting
with each other, where people's lives involve complex interactions. To
attempt to isolate a single causal mechanism does violence to the complexity of our social world.

Conclusion

These are all major objections, particularly in relation to experimental
designs, rather than quasi-experimental designs. Of course, you do not
have to agree with these objections. It is important to appreciate, furthermore, that *all* methodologies may be subject to criticisms from other
standpoints. The problem with experiments, perhaps, is that they have
been the subject of excessive claims on the part of their advocates, and
excessive criticism on the part of their detractors.

Do these criticisms suggest experiments should be abandoned? Not
really. What is important is to recognize both the strengths and weaknesses of any research design in relation to the problem at hand. Some of
the fundamental principles of the experimental design are rather important. For example, if we are seeking to measure outcomes, it is necessary
to have some means to measure change. Likewise, if we are to have reasons to believe that the independent variable had an impact, we need to
be able to compare outcomes of the E group with the C group.

As for quasi-experimental designs, they suffer less from the baggage
of excessive claims. There is recognition that the design has flaws, but
the design produces data of a sort that, in principle, provide reasons to
believe that a particular form of intervention will be efficacious (where,
of course, the results go in the right direction). If we are to recognize, for
example, that there will pretty well always be confounding factors, and

we can recognize them, we can nevertheless use findings based on these methods, as knowledge applicable to, and appropriately informing, the conduct of practice.

Exercises

6.1 Some issues that can be discussed after reading this chapter

- What are: variables, dependent variables, independent variables, hypotheses, experimental groups and control groups?
- Describe the basic characteristics of an experiment.
- What is a randomized controlled trial?
- Identify the key technical elements of an experiment.
- What is a quasi-experimental design? When should it be used, and how does it differ from an experimental design?
- What are the requirements for a causal relationship?
- State the central criticisms made of experimental designs.

6.2 An exercise in appraising and using research

Consider one of the following papers that use an experimental design (or choose one from the list on the next page):

Nicol, A.R., Smith, J., Kay, B., Hall, D., Barlow, J. and Williams, B. (1988) 'A focused casework approach to the treatment of child abuse: A controlled comparison.' *Journal of Child Psychology and Psychiatry* 29, 5, 703–711.

Norbeck, J., De Joseph, J. and Smith, R.T. (1996) 'A randomized trial of an empirically derived social support intervention to prevent low birthweight among African American women.' *Social Science and Medicine 43*, 6, 947–954.

Consider this paper in the light of a critical appraisal of experimental designs as a method of informing practice:

- Outline the background to the study and problem formulation.

- Why did the authors consider the experiment to be the best way to obtain the information sought?

- Examine the methods used. How well do they guard against threats to internal and external validity?

- What are the findings? Are there any gaps?

- What are the conclusions to the study? Are they justified by the evidence? Do the authors identify limits to the study?

- How useful is the study for practice?

Examples of research employing experimental or quasi-experimental designs

Corney, R. and Clare, A. (1983) 'The effectiveness of attached social workers in the management of depressed women in general practice.' *British Journal of Social Work 13*, 1, 57–74.

Gourney, K. (1991) 'The base for exposure treatment in agoraphobia: Some indicators for nurse therapists and community psychiatric nurses.' *Journal of Advanced Nursing 16*, 1, 82–91.

Huth, M., Broome, M., Musatto, K. and Morgan, S. (2003) 'A study of the effectiveness of a pain management education booklet for parents having cardiac surgery.' *Pain Management Nursing 4*, 1, 31–39.

Johnson, J., Fieler, V., Wlasowicz, G., Mitchell, M. and Jones, L. (1997) 'The effects of nursing care guided by self regulation theory on coping with radiation therapy.' *Oncology Nursing Forum 24*, 6, 1041–1050.

Johnson, Z., Howell, F. and Molloy, B. (1993) 'Community mothers' programme: Randomised control trial of non professional intervention in parenting.' *British Medical Journal 306*, 1449–1452.

Further reading

Bailey, K.D. (1994) *Methods of Social Research.* New York: Free Press.

Boruch, R.F. (1997) *Randomised Experiments for Planning and Evaluation: A Practical Guide.* London: Sage.

Cook, T. and Campbell, D. (1978) *Quasi Experimentation: Design and Analysis Issues for Field Settings.* Chicago: Rand McNally.

Kirk, R.E. (1995) *Experimental Design: Procedures for the Behavioural Sciences.* London: Brooks, Cole.

Pawson, R. and Tilley, N. (1997) *Realistic Evaluation.* London: Sage. (See Chapter 2.)

Rubin, A. and Babbie, E. (2001) *Research Methods for Social Work* (4th edn). Belmont, CA: Wadsworth/Thomson.

CHAPTER SEVEN

The Qualitative Interview

The qualitative interview as a strategy

Interviewing is a core method of qualitative research. It is generally referred to as a 'conversation with a purpose'. The key element of conversation is relevant because it is specifically through the mode of
conversation between researcher and researched that the data upon
which the research findings will eventually be written can be gained. We
are interested in the person's account of their situation, circumstances,
feelings and perceptions in relation to the particular research question
with which we are concerned. The nature of the data gained, therefore,
are what the person actually tells us. We are seeking to gain a qualitative
description (i.e. one couched in words and phrases) of key aspects of the
individual's social life with which we are concerned.

What we seek will differ according to the focus of the research.
Thus, for example, we may be asking any of the following kinds of
questions:

- Why do women subject to domestic violence by their
  partners nevertheless remain with those partners?

- How do older people experience general practitioner care?

- How do women suffering from depression experience social
  work intervention for purposes of child protection?

- Why do teenage women self-harm?

Each of these questions focuses on profoundly different areas of social life. However, when the method of the qualitative interview is used, it enables us to obtain data from the perception of the participants themselves on the area about which we are concerned.

We can look at this conversation-with-a-purpose in at least three ways:

- as an information-gathering exercise

- as an exercise in the creation of meaning

- as both the above, but also as a social situation with its own expectations.

It can be seen as primarily an *information-gathering exercise.* Here we see participants as the repository of information that can be imparted to us and that will give us an idea of what they are about. They enable us to know, for example, how they experience something. If we are looking, for example, to find out how individuals experience health or social work intervention, then we could ask them about this. The information provided could be used – as it frequently is – as a significant element of the evaluation of human services in both health and social work. Where, for example, clients report that they feel they are given little time, they feel demeaned by practitioners, or that practitioners listen to them very little, then we may conclude that the service needs improving. You may suggest that this is just the perspective of the client, but the response might be that it is for them, after all, that the service is developed, so it is to them that we need to respond. The information is treated as if it has some objectivity – that it represents a real and valid way of presenting the situation. It is an objective report on the world – this is 'how the clients feel about the intervention'.

Another way of viewing the interview is not as a straightforward information-generating exercise at all, rather as an *exercise in the creation of meaning.* Here we see the participants as people who seek to create a narrative to account for their experiences of the world. It is literally the 'creation of a story', a perspective on the world, no more no less. What an individual will do is report on the situation as they see it, a perspective constructed by themselves. The woman who talks of her reasons for staying with her violent husband may state that he doesn't really mean it; that he is a sad person, and always regrets it afterwards. He suffers, she may say, from low self-esteem, and finds himself lashing out when he feels he is being put down. Indeed, it is to a large extent her fault, since she goads him by standing her ground with him – perhaps it is she who is really to blame. Of course, from the perspective of another person, he may be a callous, manipulative individual, playing on her better nature. But for her, she has been able to construct a particular meaning out of the situation, from which she is able to justify and make sense of remaining with him.

Another way of viewing the interview allows for both the above points, but recognizes that the interview itself is a particular kind of *social situation with its own expectations* which help to govern how it occurs. The interview has a dynamic of its own, in that it is a role relationship, in which there is one person in the role of interviewer, another in the role of respondent, and a purpose (at least one) to gather information, discover meanings, and so on. Although it is about gaining an account from the subject, it has a dynamic of its own, based on the fact that each person has a perception of what it is about, and is, so to speak, 'playing out' the scenario (that of the research interview). It is like playing out a scene in a play. Although the overall purpose is understood, generally, by all those taking part, the 'agenda' of the respondent may not be exactly what the researcher has in mind. They may, for example, wish to 'impression manage' the situation (i.e. their motivation will be to give a particular kind of impression of themselves to the interviewer). If we are interviewing carers of older people, they may wish to present us with a view of themselves as essentially caring individuals, and their responses will be designed to encourage that perception. They may wish to be economical with the truth – research with drug dealers may not, for example, lead to entirely forthright answers, particularly as a high level of trust may be required for imparting that information, and such trust may be very difficult to generate within the context of the research interview. Thus the research interview becomes, metaphorically, a 'stage' in which those present act out particular roles with each other. Of course, this has profound implications for the nature of information gained, and how it is to be presented in the research findings.

Interviewing versus other methods

Qualitative interviewing is not the only method of gaining research information, but it can do certain things particularly well.

The qualitative interview can enable us to probe the inner motivation and reasons for the way people may be acting. It works best perhaps where what we are seeking is not amenable to simple observation. We have already given the example of the woman who stays with her violent partner, an example that fits with exactly this approach. Here we are able to understand her reasoning behind her decision to stay with this partner (that he is really a rather sad man, with low self-esteem, who doesn't ever intend to be violent, and 'anyway it is, to a great degree, my fault'). There are few other ways to provide a better insight into reasons for acting than the interview. We could, for example, seek to observe the two individuals interacting with each other. However, even here we may only be able to infer at best why they are doing what they are doing. We can see what they are doing, but we can't see why they are.

The qualitative interview can enable us to understand not just single events or actions, but the ways in which these are linked together. Where, for example, we are looking at particular kinds of responses to the demands of child care, we can explore development, continuity and change over time. We may be interested, for example, in the ways in which a woman has sought to respond differently to the challenges she is experiencing from her teenage son. She may have responded initially through corporal punishment, gone through a process of reasoning and now sought to get relief through letting him stay at his aunt's for extended periods. Where we seek to understand the development of these processes we are best placed to do so through the medium of the interview.

The qualitative interview can enable us to obtain information about the judgements individuals make about their situations. We can, for example, explore where women see there are reasons to feel optimistic about their future with regard to caring for their children, even though they are subject to child protection intervention. Or whether carers of people suffering from schizophrenia feel they will be able to continue support, and whether they need support. Likewise, we can explore whether they feel they have been fairly treated by health or social services when seeking help, for example, with housing, health or welfare difficulties. We can also explore judgements about their situation after, for example, traumatic news, such as learning that their partner has cancer.

The key to all this is (a) that the information obtained is not simply obtainable through direct observation (we need something of the person's account of the situation to answer the kinds of questions we present) and (b) that we wish to gain deeper understanding than is to be obtained merely by the restricted responses allowed in quantitative questionnaires. The interview (qualitative) allows a deeper level of exploration than would be otherwise available of the perceptions, motivations, judgements, and so on, of the individuals who are being interviewed.

Interviews can be viewed as information gathering, the creation of meaning, or as events in themselves with their own dynamics.

Types of interview

At least three types of interview can be identified:

- standardized/structural interviews
- unstandardized interviews
- semi-standardized interviews.

Standardized/structured interviews

This uses a formally structured schedule of interview questions, a list of which is possessed by the interviewer. The interviewer goes through these one by one, and seeks to get answers to them. We can give an example of the kind of thing we mean by drawing on a list of questions produced by Berg (2000, p.69). This one relates to finding out information about a diet history:

1. When is the first time you eat or drink on a typical day?

2. What is the first thing you eat?

3. When is the next time you eat or drink?

4. What do you eat or drink?

5. When is the next time that you eat or drink?

6. What do you eat or drink?

7. What else do you eat or drink on a typical day?

8. How many times a week do you eat eggs? cheese? milk? fish? beef? pork? beans? corn? grits? bread? cereal? ice cream? fruits? vegetables?

9. Which protein foods do you like best?

10. Which protein foods do you not eat?

11. Which foods do you like between meals?

In general, fully structured questionnaires are part of a quantitative methodology, where you are identifying the number of times this, that or the other occurs. In this case, there is some scope for a qualitative response to at least some of the questions, but it is clear that it is quite circumscribed. As a qualitative methodology, it is quite limited, and allows very little exploration of the details of the individual's approach to their diet. What, for example, prompts their decision to eat in certain ways?

What are their health beliefs? Are they informed by these beliefs in deciding about their diet, or does this not concern them? There is little that this can produce except a description of what they do (in terms of eating) rather than how what they do is informed by sets of beliefs or attitudes, or lifestyle choices.

The rationale with this approach is that they are offering the respondent pretty well the same set of topics and questions, and that, as a result, there will, it is believed, be a certain amount of standardization between different respondents. This gives, according to the advocates of this method, a crucial consistency in the way the researcher treats the respondent, and hence gives greater rigour to the research process.

- Researchers using this approach have fairly solid ideas about the things they want to uncover during interviews. They assume the questions are sufficiently comprehensive to elicit nearly all the information relevant to the subject.

- They further assume that all questions have been worded in a manner that allows subjects to understand clearly what they are being asked – that is, written in a way that makes equal sense to all of them.

- Finally they assume that each question's meaning is identical for each subject. It doesn't matter if they come from different cultures (if, for example, we interview across cultures), the meaning will be the same.

Of course where these assumptions do not hold up, there may be grounds for suggesting that apparently informative research findings are, in fact, nothing of the kind, and reflect only the confusion generated by the original questions.

Unstandardized interviews

The unstandardized interview is undertaken with only a set of general areas that are the concern of the researcher. Where, for example, we are interested in working-class women's understanding of health and illness, and how they should respond to them, although we have these as general areas, the unstandardized interviewer will only, at the outset, adopt the most general areas to focus on. They may, for example, simply start with two or three areas which they wish to explore:

- women's perceptions of health and illness

- women's perceptions of appropriate responses to health and illness issues

- women's perception of others' views in their community about the above two, and how these affect them.

Why this approach? The point is that it assumes that we actually can know very little about this subject before we start, and that, therefore, it is best to make as few assumptions as possible before beginning research. If we prepare too many questions in advance, this will assume that our pre-existing perceptions of what is important are generally accurate. Yet, this is the one thing, according to this methodology, that we cannot know until after we have got the responses from the subjects. This means that we 'discover' what is important – the important themes, questions and issues – during the process of interviewing. This emerges as part of a conversation with the subjects, and in the process of the conversation we explore important or salient issues that emerge.

These researchers, in other words, seek to assume as little as possible at the outset of the research, and seek to be increasingly guided by the information they are given. Another important point is that researchers assume, unlike with standardized interviews, that not all subjects will find the same meaning in similarly worded questions – that the same question will not necessarily have the same meaning to person A as it has to person B.

This last point reflects the way these researchers generally see the social world. The social world is not a place where we can assume that we all share the same understanding of different things. For example, it may be the case that what constitutes 'good health' for a middle-class woman may not be the same as it is for a working-class man. If I am a middle-class female researcher, and if I draw up a set of questions reflecting my understanding of healthy behaviour, I may entirely miss the point if I am researching into the health beliefs of a working-class man.

In an unstandardized interview, therefore, the interviewer must develop, adapt and generate questions and follow up probes (i.e. exploring in more detail the content of a participant's responses) appropriate to the given situation and general purpose of the investigation. According to this view, this results in appropriate and relevant questions arising from the interactions (between participant and researcher) during the interview itself.

Unstandardized interviews are used by those who wish to assume the least possible amount about the people being studied before they actually find things out. They can also be used when the researcher is insufficiently familiar with key elements of the research area, or the lives of those who are being researched (e.g. different religions, cultures, ethnic groups, class etc.). Thus they are used:

- not only to generate findings
- but also to generate the questions/areas for study themselves.

Semi-standardized interviews

Between the standardized and unstandardized interview lies the semi-standardized interview. This involves implementing a number of predetermined questions or themes. On the one hand, there is a set of questions that can be asked. On the other hand, this approach does not prevent – indeed it generally encourages – the development of themes within those areas through probing questions. These additional questions, not scripted beforehand, emerge out of the interview itself, or the conversation occurring around the predetermined questions or themes.

An example of a semi-structured interview approach comes from my own large-scale study of depressed mothers in child and family care (Sheppard 2001). I was interested in how the social workers responded to the particular problems and needs presented by families with depressed mothers, and particularly the mother herself. The issue was significant because in most families it is the mother who is the first and last best hope for the children, and depression can have a very disabling effect on (a) their capacity to parent and (b) their capacity to resolve their problems. We interviewed both mothers and social workers twice. In the second interview with the social workers, for example, we focused on some broad areas. These broad areas, in turn, it was expected, would enable us to begin to draw out further themes so that we would be able to explore key aspects of practice that we might not have anticipated at the outset to be of significance. Hence the questions we asked were:

1. What are the main reasons that social services are involved with this family?

2. What are the main problems in this family and why do you think they have them?

3. In the work undertaken with this family, what have you done and why have you done it?

4. To what extent have you been able to draw on the mother and her opinions in developing your practice strategies with the family?

5. How influential has the mother been in developing the direction of practice?

Now these were general questions allowing us an entrée into these broad areas. However, for example, on the questions (4 and 5) focusing on working with the mother, it emerged sometimes that some women were perceived as 'obstructive'. In that case, we could follow up with further questions on this: How was she being obstructive? How did you try to deal with this? How successful were you in this? These questions are called prompts. These questions were not determined in advance but emerged during the course of the interview. Thus, we had a mixture of predetermined and responsive questions, through which the information emerged.

Thus we can see that questions are typically asked of each interviewee in a systematic and consistent order, but the interviewers are allowed the freedom to explore – they are expected to probe far beyond the answers to their prepared and standardized questions.

There are nevertheless assumptions underlying this approach:

- If questions are to be standardized they must be formulated in words familiar to the people being interviewed.

- Which relates to the second point: Questions used in semi-standardized interviews can reflect awareness that individuals understand the world in differing ways.

Interviews can have a greater or lesser amount of detail in their initial questions. Those which seek to provide the greatest scope for exploration with interviewees are unstandardized, or unstructured, interviews.

Interview schedule development

What to include in the questionnaire

There has to be a clear relationship between the topic we wish to study and the interview schedule developed. Thus we can have a particular overall topic or question, and then a number of areas which we wish to focus upon. Our general focus might be on the practice strategies of social workers with depressed mothers. We then begin with an outline of the main or broad categories that we feel may be relevant for the study – which enables us to visualize the categories relevant for the study. From this, essential questions can emerge concerning the central focus of the study. These are geared towards the specifically desired information.

We might be interested in: social workers' definitions of need, how they understand the nature of depression and the impact this has on the ways they view the women; the extent to which partnership is manifested in the conduct of intervention; and the basic intervention strategies they use. However, research can be as much about what is not included as what is included. We would need to be aware of things that are missed out, because that shows the limits to the research – and what might even be termed its bias.

In this case, for example, we might suggest that a failure to interview the women, to determine their perception of intervention strategy, left out a crucial element of the 'picture'. In fact, in my research, this did not happen, but if we had failed to look at the women's perceptions, it would to that extent be limited, or even biased (to a professional construction) of the particular area studied.

Likewise, for example, suppose we were to focus upon whether or not improvements were made with particular kinds of practice strategies. If we sought only the views of social workers, we would not have any idea about the experiences of the women themselves. What if, for example, the social workers said there had been a clear improvement, but the women's own experience did not reflect this? Or what if the social workers were judging improvement solely in terms of the ways the child care or child behaviour had improved, but the women themselves were as concerned with the ways they felt?

In this case there would be separate agendas: one would be the agenda of the social worker focusing on the child (and that would be their criterion) and the other about the woman focusing on herself (as well), which would be an alternative criterion.

Probing

As already mentioned, probes provide the researcher with a way of drawing out a more complete story from their respondent. Researchers frequently ask their participants to elaborate on what they have already answered in response to a question (e.g. 'Can you tell me about that?' or 'How long did you have that?').

Here is an example from my study of prevention and coping in child and family care (Sheppard 2004). This research sought to examine how mothers coped in adversity with child and parenting problems, in particular when they had been refused social service support. Here we are asking a mother about what support the mother gets with child care. The mother has identified a few people who help out.

Researcher: Do you feel that people like Tracey, Janet and your mum have helped?

Woman: Oh yes, definitely. I mean I'm a speaker and I need to speak about things, and I'll just go over. The main one is Tracey, couldn't get Janet down from Scotland. But I phoned her, and my mum's here, but Tracey usually gets sent over. They have helped definitely.

Researcher [probing]: So she gives you emotional support? Can you give me an example?

Woman: Just then, she's just there when I need her, do you know? If I need to speak mainly, I need to speak to someone, or if I ask her to keep an eye on the kids whilst I go out looking for Lucy, or else I ask Tracey if I can use your phone to phone the police…and she's just, you know, she's just there.

Engaging the interviewees

One of the key elements in all this is the extent to which we are able to engage participants in the interview process. How can we get their enthusiasm to be involved? How can we maintain their interest when they are involved? How can we generate trust so they feel confident to talk to us about the issues of concern? These are key factors in seeking to get the most accurate and comprehensive work done.

GETTING PEOPLE INVOLVED/MAKING YOURSELF ACCEPTABLE

Berg (2000) describes the attempts of an individual to engage people from a community so that they could get a group who could match a sample of patients in a manic depressive study. The fact that this was not about qualitative research is less important than what it tells us about engaging people. The interviewer sought to engage people in the research, yet despite his best efforts, which included dressing himself in a way which was highly acceptable to the cultural groups of that area, he was unable to get a positive response from a single person all day long. Indeed, in the majority of homes people refused even to answer him.

He discovered subsequently that the neighbourhood had been subject to a spate of burglaries recently and, furthermore, an advisory film, seen through neighbourhood watch, indicated that burglars were likely to take on a persona that enabled them to mingle relatively easily in any area they aimed for. They would seek, therefore, to be indistinguishable from those who lived in the area. The researcher's efforts to be just that actually made him the focus for suspicion.

In the end he came across a local judge who said he should approach the neighbourhood watch, drop his name, and he would get a better response – which he did!

KNOWING THE LANGUAGE OF THE SUBJECTS

Social research can involve a wide range of cultures and groups, and they may use different words and phrases from those of the researcher. Where they do, there is liable to be a gap between researcher and interviewee that makes it less likely that they will be able to ask the right questions, make appropriate prompts and gain the most comprehensive information. An obvious example these days is that of working-class black male youth culture. It is not difficult to envisage middle-aged, middle-class white researchers might find it difficult to engage such black youths without a considerable effort to gain quite detailed knowledge of their culture, interests and expressions.

RECOGNIZING SENSITIVE ASPECTS OF RESEARCH

One of the key elements of research with certain groups is that, in order both to gain acceptance and to maximize the possibility of an honest and comprehensive response, membership of that group is necessary. I am particularly aware of this, since a large proportion of my research has involved mothers in adversity. This is not a group of which I can easily claim membership, and my direct involvement in face-to-face interviews could be seen to be a problem. It is quite likely that: (a) if I did seek to be the primary researcher, many women would refuse to be involved, and (b) even where they agreed, they may be more guarded than would be the case where a woman interviewed them.

I have always, therefore, made sure that the primary researchers have been women and, while we have been honest about my position as Director of Research, this has not proved an impediment to the participants. This suggests that the most significant element for them is whom they are actually talking to.

Why should this be the case? Well, we have worked on the assumption that women share a certain world and certain assumptions. Women are more likely to feel able to disclose information about themselves to other women because they feel they are more likely to be understood. This points to a key issue in research in health and social work: that we are often researching highly sensitive areas where people need to feel understood when giving out sensitive information about their lives and their family.

When you are dealing with sensitive issues, many of the professional concerns relevant to the health professional, counsellor or social worker come to the fore. The need to be understood and the need to feel empathy means that some, at least, of the basic characteristics of the therapeutic interview come into play. The capacity to listen, to respond to feelings and to know how they feel is very important for the researcher. The woman, feeling confident that she is understood, is more likely to give more information, and more detailed information than otherwise.

PUBLIC AND PRIVATE ACCOUNTS

Jocelyn Cornwell (1984) takes matters further than this. She was interviewing working-class men and women – predominantly women – about their health experiences. She argued that the conventional approach of doing one interview per person, even if it were relatively long, was not appropriate and would not get accurate information. She placed great importance on the relationship with interviewees, and had many interviews with each of the 24 participants over a lengthy period of time.

She distinguished between public and private accounts. Public accounts were accounts designed to be tailored to be acceptable to people in a public context. They would be less controversial, less deep, and less likely to give away more personal facets of themselves. Private accounts spring directly from the personal experience of the individuals and the thoughts and feelings that accompany them.

The idea with the repeat interviews was that Cornwell would build up a personal relationship with these people, and thus be more likely to get at their private accounts. This, according to Cornwell, would yield more meaningful and useful data, without exploiting the subjects. Quite what these people thought about being multiply interviewed by Cornwell, I am not sure. One cannot be sure that, in a fit of desperation, they would not say: 'Tell me what you want, I'll give it to you – just leave me alone!'

> Engaging the interviewee involves not simply gaining access, but approaching them in such a way, or with particular interviewer characteristics, that enables the most complete responses on their part.

Focus groups

Focus group interviews are, like individual interviews, generally qualitative. However, instead of involving a one-to-one interviewer–subject relationship, they involve a group of people, generally recommended to be between six and twelve (some think six to eight is the optimum size).

They too are conversations with a (research) purpose, but the conversations generally go on between group members, rather than interviewer to interviewee. The key to the distinctive nature of focus groups is the way in which group interaction – the way in which members of the group talk to each other, and discuss the subject about which the research is concerned – actually leads to obtaining data.

What are they used for? Well, they are big in market research, and also frequently used in social research. In market research, and sometimes in social research, they are used as 'add-ons' to survey methods. They may be used in the early stages of a large survey study. Prior to the drafting and piloting of a survey instrument, focus groups can be used to make sure the kinds of issues identified, and the kinds of language used, reflects the target group of the research. So if we were interested in surveying young black people about racial harassment, we could use focus groups to identify key issues, and identify appropriate language, so the instrument made sense to them. Alternatively, they could be used to help interpret survey results. For example, when fear is expressed about catching AIDS through 'donating' blood, it can turn out that respondents do not distinguish between donating and receiving blood.

What can focus groups do, then? Well they are, in some respects, an efficient way of getting qualitative data from (relatively) large numbers of people. If you have a focus group of six for one hour, then you have six times the respondents of a one-hour individual interview. However, you also lose the direct one-to-one element.

It is not really about size, so much as what they can offer. They offer many of the advantages of individual interviews – flexibility, probing, depth (potentially). However, it is in the capacity of the group members to interact with each other, to discuss matters between themselves, that focus groups gain their unique advantage. It is a socially oriented research procedure. People are social creatures who interact with others. They are influenced by the comments of others, and make decisions after listening to advice from people around them (well, sometimes they do!).

Focus groups place people in 'real-life' situations (in this respect), as opposed to, for example, the controlled experimental situation. Also, in one-to-one qualitative interviews, you do not capture the dynamic nature of the group interaction – the exchange of ideas, the stimulus to new ideas, the sense of a number of you engaging in a similar enterprise. Rather than two people, one questioning, the other answering, you have the opportunity for debate, which can extend and develop the ideas of individuals comprising the group.

It can go further than that. The focus group can provide the opportunity for articulating assumptions that are not usually articulated. The group may, for example, be discussing their attitudes to mental illness, and in the process begin to identify what it is that they think of as mentally ill behaviour. We may, for example, have some people saying that it is behaviour that is 'weird', but others in the group may ask what they mean by weird. They might then provide an account of behaviour that was weird, which might then be followed by similar accounts by others. They would then be in a position, through these series of examples, to identify exactly what was meant by 'weird' and how this varied across different circumstances.

It is, in this respect, the occasion for group members to engage in what has been called 'retrospective introspection' – that is examining their previously held ideas and thinking about how and why they held them. Of course, the teasing out of the ideas may be only partial, and there may be areas of ambiguity, but it is clearly in the opportunity for interaction with other participants and in discussing their ideas that qualitatively oriented focus groups can make their unique offering.

The role of the interviewer with the focus group is rather different from the one-to-one interview. In a sense, the purposes are similar – to get the perspectives, views and meanings of participants. However, the way this is achieved is different. Instead of an interviewer directly asking questions of each member, he or she is seeking to facilitate group interaction, with a view to obtaining the kinds of information being sought. As with psychotherapeutic groups, the overall aim is for 'the group to do the work'.

The researcher, then, is seeking to find ways to encourage the group to hold discussions that will help them obtain the information they want. Hence much of their work will be designed as 'invitations' to participate.

They might, for example, find one person strongly expressing a view. The facilitator might then say: 'What do other people think about that?' The idea here is to stimulate others to be involved. The question leaves others to respond as they see fit, without the researcher leading them. This could lead to widespread agreement, or disagreement. In either case, but particularly the latter, the opportunity for examining and developing deeper understandings of perspectives becomes apparent.

If, for example, we are researching with men who have committed acts of domestic violence, we might find some men suggesting that the women think such violence is appropriate, and that it presents them with boundaries. They might also suggest that the women were not hurt very much anyway, or that it was a man's place to discipline his wife. These views, repugnant as they are, when out in the open in a group, can stimulate discussion that can help us understand the deeper meanings and motivations for these acts of violence. We may begin to understand the implicit view of women as, in some respects, 'property', or as needing 'disciplining' because they are liable to get hysterical and manifest irrational behaviour. These deeper meanings of 'property ownership' and 'irrationality' would then emerge from the initial view of the need to discipline and set boundaries, and perceived women's 'compliance'.

It is in the capacity of the group members to interact with each other, to discuss matters between themselves, that focus groups gain their unique advantage. It is a socially oriented research procedure.

Conclusion

The qualitative interview is in widespread use in qualitative research, and is in many respects fundamental to that research form. Just as more qualitative methods contain assumptions, so do these form of interviews (and they may just as much be subject to criticism from those of opposing views). The emphasis on meaning construction, so often central to the qualitative interview, and particularly the very open form of unstandardized interviewing, may be criticized as 'unscientific' by some quantitative researchers.

Some even question the nature of 'knowledge' generated. It may be that such methods are considered closer to journalism than to real scientific research (indeed that may be a criticism that would not be wholly unwelcome to some qualitative researchers who do not wish to see themselves as scientists in any conventional sense). The very open nature of the interview questions, for those of a more quantitative disposition, lays qualitative interviewers open to the criticism of 'bias' and inconsistency, which, for some, would render findings useless. However, for many qualitative researchers this so-called inconsistency reflects the reality of social life – that different people will have different issues and concerns, that they will express them differently, and that, as a result, they should be approached in a way that is sensitive to those differences. Far from being a disadvantage, this process is more likely to present more meaningful findings.

The interview, then, is a key part of qualitative methodology. Another is the use of observation, particularly participant observation, techniques. These are a key part of ethnography, to which we will turn next.

Exercises

7.1 Some issues that can be discussed after reading this chapter

- What is a 'conversation with a purpose'? What are the different ways in which this can be used?

- What particular qualities do qualitative interviews bring to social research?

- Describe different types of interview. What are their strengths and weaknesses?

- What is the significance of interviewee or participant engagement?

- What are public and private accounts?

- What are focus groups? When should they be used?

7.2 An exercise using qualitative interviewing

The aim is to introduce readers to the practicality of research interviewing through:

- developing a semi-structured interview schedule

- acting it out as an interview

- analysing the process

- the group observing, and those participating, commenting on questions and probes, analysing key elements, including substantive elements, particularly in the light of their own experience.

This should be done in a group. It should involve one participant (the interviewee) and at least one interviewer (although there could be two or three). It is a good idea to have some others watching. An appropriate venue for this is the seminar.

The task for the group conducting the interview 'role play' could focus on any issue of their choice. In the case of professional health and social work students, an appropriate topic would be the experience of students entering and engaging their practice placement. This would involve the following elements:

- the identification of three to five key themes and questions to ask the interviewee

- carrying out the interview, involving the key themes and questions, and prompts at key moments
- the whole group observing and commenting on this process, analysing key elements, including substantive elements, particularly in the light of personal experiences
- participants commenting on questions and probes.

Examples of research employing qualitative interviews

Bruner, D. and Boyd, C. (1999) 'Assessing women's sexuality after cancer therapy: Checking assumptions with the focus group technique.' *Cancer Nursing 22*, 6, 438–447.

Ferrell, B., Chu, D., Wagman, L., Juarez, G., Borrneman, T., Cullinane, C. and McCahill, L. (2003) 'Patient and surgeon decision making regarding surgery for advanced cancer.' *Oncology Nursing Forum 30*, 6E, 106–114.

Hansen, E. (1994) 'An exploration of the taken for granted world of the cancer nurse in relation to stress and the person with cancer.' *Journal of Advanced Nursing 19*, 1, 12–20.

Schulze, B. and Angermeyer, M. (2003) 'Subjective experience of stigma: A focus group study of schizophrenic patients, their relatives, and mental health professionals.' *Social Science and Medicine 56*, 2, 299–312.

Further reading

Cohen, M.C. and Garrett, K. (1999) 'Breaking the rules: A group work perspective on focus group research.' *British Journal of Social Work 29*, 3, 359–372.

Freeman, K., O'Dell, C. and Meola, C. (2001) 'Focus group methodology for patients, parents and siblings.' *Journal of Pediatric Oncology Nursing 18*, 6, 276–286.

Gillham, B. (2000) *The Research Interview.* London and New York: Continuum.

Greenbaum, T. (1998) *The Handbook for Focus Group Research.* London: Sage.

Kvale, S. (1996) *Interviews: An Introduction to Qualitative Research Interviews.* London: Sage.

McCracken, G. (1989) *The Long Interview.* London: Sage.

Morgan, D. (1993) *Successful Focus Groups.* London: Sage.

Morgan, D. (1997) *Focus Groups as Qualitative Research.* London: Sage.

Silverman, D. (ed) (2004) *Qualitative Research: Theory, Method and Practice: Part 4.* London: Sage.

CHAPTER EIGHT
Ethnography and Practice

Suppose you wanted to have some idea of the details of the kinds of interactions between family centre workers and users, or between patients and staff in a hospital. You may be concerned because you wanted to develop the best kind of environment for the users of the service. You are interested in the detail, the processes by which staff and users, or health workers and patients, are able to get on.

What, you might wonder, are the kinds of things that are important in enabling users/patients to feel welcome? What are the factors that create a positive dialogue between staff and patients/users? How can you ensure that those using the service, such as a day centre or family centre, actually want to participate fully? How can you make things consumer-friendly and democratic?

Well as noted before, you can observe the situations yourself, and ask people involved. These are important. You could instead call upon studies of similar institutions that provide some insight into the kinds of issues that might arise, and the kinds of circumstances in which they arise. These studies would be concerned with the minutiae of social interaction, with the details of day-to-day contact. The very depth and detail of the studies can bring to light factors that may be relevant to your situation, and may help guide you in amendments and developments. These could relate to the way the institution is run, as well as the individual actions of those who work in it. It is concerned with the way users and workers, patients, and health professionals' everyday understanding of the world creates the context for the interactions that occur. It is also concerned with the meanings of those interactions to those taking part.

Research that focuses on these kinds of details, the minutiae of social interaction, is called ethnography, and it provides a further important dimension of social research relevant to practice.

What is ethnography?

The term 'ethnography' refers primarily to a particular method or set of methods. In its most characteristic form it involves the researcher participating, openly or covertly, in people's daily lives for an extended period of time, watching what happens, listening to what is said, asking questions – in fact collecting whatever data are available to throw light on the issues that are the focus for research. Ethnography places researchers in the midst of whatever it is that they study. From this vantage point, they seek to examine the social world as perceived by subjects/participants, and represent these observations as accounts.

The kind of thing that would qualify here would be involvement and participation in a family centre for an extended period of time; observation of police work, including going out on patrols; membership of a psychiatric ward. At times ethnographers have obtained jobs in order to carry out their observations – for example as a hospital porter in order to examine the working of the hospital. This very much involves the researcher as 'insider' (participating in the setting) as well as 'outsider' (the researcher focusing on the setting). Ethnography, then, is generally about observation, although interviews and the use of documents can accompany this, as a means of gaining detailed answers to research questions.

Some researchers describe the ethnographic process as 'subjective soaking' – this occurs when the researcher abandons the idea of objectivity or scientific neutrality and attempts to merge into the culture being studied.

So, what are the key features of the ethnographic method?

- People's behaviour is studied in everyday contexts, rather than experimental conditions created by the researcher.

- Data are gathered from a range of sources, but observations and relatively informal conversations are usually the main data-gathering techniques.

- The approach to data collection is usually unstructured in the sense that it does not involve following through a detailed plan set up at the beginning. Nor are the categories used for interpreting what people say and do predetermined and fixed. This does not mean that the research is unsystematic – merely that initially the data are collected in as wide a front as possible.

- The focus is usually a single setting or group, and is of relatively small scale.

- The analysis of the data involves interpretation of the meaning and functions of human actions, and mainly take the form of verbal descriptions and explanations.

As a set of methods, ethnography is not far removed from the sort of approach that we all use in everyday life to make sense of our surroundings.

> The heart of ethnography is its attempt to reproduce or present the subjective perception of subjects'/participants' social world.

Assumptions underlying ethnography

Ethnographers are generally committed to a number of positions:

- naturalism

- understanding

- discovery.

NATURALISM

This is the view that the aim of social research is to capture the character of naturally occurring human behaviour, and that it can only be achieved by first-hand contact with it, *not* by inferences from what people do in artificial settings like experiments, or from what they say in interviews about what they do elsewhere. Another implication of this is that the researcher should seek to minimize his or her effect on the behaviour of the people being studied. The aim of this is to increase the chances that what is discovered in the setting will be generalizable to other similar settings.

UNDERSTANDING

Central here is the argument that human actions differ from the behaviour of physical objects. People do not consist simply of fixed responses, but their perceptions and actions involve interpretation of the social world around them, and the construction of responses (i.e. the creation of responses with certain meanings attached to them).

Sometimes this argument reflects the complete rejection of the concept of causality as inapplicable to the social world. Causality involves human behaviour being 'caused' by some external forces – and it is this that is rejected. There is an insistence that human actions are freely constructed and voluntary – determined by the individuals themselves, who are able to give reasons for what they do and understand them in particular ways.

From this point of view, if we are to explain or describe human actions effectively, we need to gain an understanding of the cultural perspectives on which they are based. Ethnographers, therefore, argue that it is necessary to learn the culture of the group one is studying before one can produce valid descriptions or explanations for the behaviour of members. This is the reason for the centrality of participant observation and unstructured interviewing to ethnographic method.

DISCOVERY

Another feature is a perception of the research process as discovery – or inductive-based – rather than being limited to the testing of hypotheses. It is argued that if one approaches social life with a set of hypotheses, one may fail to discover the true nature of that which is being studied, since we are blinded by the assumptions built into the hypotheses.

Instead we should begin our research with minimal assumptions, so as to maximize our capacity for learning. For this reason, ethnographers rarely begin their research with specific hypotheses. Rather they have a general interest in some areas of social life. The focus of the research is narrowed and sharpened, and perhaps even changed substantially, as it proceeds.

Research design – access

Because of the ethnographer's close involvement through direct observation of the social setting or group with which they are concerned, the problem of gaining access to the setting or group, and hence the data, looms very large. Actually this is an issue of wide interest for social work research generally, not simply confined to those few who take an ethnographic approach. The nature of research in health and social work generally means gaining access to settings or populations. This has been the case with most of my research – for example, when carrying out work on mental health social workers' approach to mental health work, compared with community psychiatric nurses, there was a protracted period of negotiation before I could even gain access to the setting through which research could take place (Sheppard 1991).

The issue of gaining access is often at its most acute in the initial negotiations to gain access to a setting, and during the early period of research 'in the field' (as ethnographers call it). But the problem persists, to some extent or other, throughout the data-collection period. The fact that you are there amongst people who may not be entirely clear about what you are doing, or who harbour fears about the outcome of the findings, can make engagement with the people and setting difficult. These issues have all emerged very strongly in all my research, although this has involved not only some observation, but extensive interviewing. In many ways, gaining access is a thoroughly practical issue, and involves drawing on the interpersonal resources of the researcher. These include their charm, sense of trustworthiness, responsiveness, recognition of what research subjects or participants may be concerned with, and so on.

Question: How far does the issue of access in research affect the usefulness of findings for practice?

Gatekeepers

The process of gaining and maintaining access can have profound implications for the nature of the research you are able to undertake. Those who are able to grant access to a research site are called 'gatekeepers'. In formal organizations, such as health or social services departments, access negotiations may be focused on official permission that can be granted or withheld by key personnel. These key personnel – generally at some managerial level – become the initial point of contact.

Examples of their significance can be given from my research. In the main study of social work practice with depressed mothers (Sheppard 2001) the three sites studied went through different processes. In one authority, the decision had been made at the very highest level (Director/Council Social Services Committee), but with little consultation with the teams actually involved. Thus when I went to meet the team, they were faced with clear instructions that involvement was part of their work task, and there was a certain degree of concern and dissatisfaction. I had to be sensitive to this, and sought to persuade them of the value of the research, which, to be fair, they generally – but not entirely – accepted. I was, though, caught off guard, unaware that the teams had not been consulted in the first place. It was mainly because of my fairly extensive experience of doing this kind of work that my unpreparedness did not lead to some potential difficulties.

Nevertheless, these teams were going to be involved because they had no choice. Another two teams, from a different local authority, were approached at lower managerial level – team manager – and the process from the start involved discussing with them the nature and purpose of the research. As a result there was a more obvious initial consensus about taking part in the research. This was the same with a third pair of teams, in another authority, that were also involved in the study.

In two of the three authorities, however, for some time there were social workers who only took part with some degree of reluctance. This, it strikes me, is something about the culture of social work. Regardless of the fact that they have heavy workloads – which they do – social workers, in higher numbers than other professions, tend to be wary of research taking place in their setting. There is a greater tendency to say 'no' first and then revise this later. With other groups with whom I have worked (e.g. health visitors) the opposite is the case ('yes' first and 'yes' later!) (Sheppard 1996, 1997a, 1998b). Indeed, there can be greater difficulty persuading those at managerial level of the usefulness of the research, than those at the 'coal face'. These features could be for various reasons; one, I suspect, is the sense of embattlement felt by social workers who consider themselves criticized far too much (with some justification). Another is, in my view, to do with suspicion of a managerial agenda, and even of being 'put upon' by managers – which gets extended to the researcher.

So we can have different 'levels' or points of entry, and responses that are affected by the culture of the organization itself, and perceptions of hidden and not-so-hidden agendas.

> The intense involvement of the researcher in the environment of those he or she studies means that the issue of access is of particular importance.

The gatekeeper will generally and understandably be concerned about the implications for the organization, group or community of carrying out the research, particularly the 'picture' the researcher will paint of it. They may well have a practical interest in seeing themselves or their colleagues in a favourable light. On the other hand – in the case of health and social services departments at any rate – being involved with research might be seen as accruing 'brownie points'. This could be from government departments, such as the Department of Health in the United Kingdom, who would see it as evidence of forward thinking, or more widely culturally, where health and social work professions could see its claims to professional status enhanced by involvement in the production of knowledge.

Their approach or attitude can have implications for research access and hence research findings. They may wish to enhance access to some areas of work or organization, while seeking to seal off others. One of the problems here is that it might be precisely the most sensitive areas that are of greatest interest to fieldworkers. In the case of social workers this has arisen in the most bizarre of ways. When I was carrying out the research on depressed mothers, one or two social workers tried to argue that we should not interview some mothers because they were *too* depressed! Indeed, as we were involved in a two-stage research process (an initial screening to discover whether they were depressed, followed up by a more detailed interview), we had already interviewed them once, *and* gained their agreement.

Question: How do gatekeepers and others affect the usefulness and applicability of findings to practice?

Insiders and outsiders

Because of the nature of the research, which involves being on site for extended periods of time, observing what is going on, asking questions and taking notes, the whole process of ethnography is highly sensitive. It is, in many respects, a very intrusive form of research, and can be experienced as such (except where the researcher keeps his identity secret, as did Goffman (1961) as hospital porter in his research). Thus the person of the researcher, and the impression the subjects get of him or her, becomes of particular importance. Again this is an issue that can facilitate or disable access to key elements of research, and thus affect findings.

People in the field will seek to locate the ethnographer within their own experience (and that experience, of any kind of research, may be non-existent, partial or limited). Where limited knowledge of research exists, some people may be highly suspicious of the 'real' intent – even the real identity – of the researchers. They may perceive them to be something else entirely – generally some kind of authority or spy figure. This can get in the way of research.

However, even the identity of an individual as a researcher can get in the way. One example from research on the Royal Ulster Constabulary in Northern Ireland identified a strong antipathy towards sociologists: 'If anything gets me down it's bloody sociology. I think it's the biggest load of shite – it's as simple as that!' (Brewer 1991, p.16). In this case sociology was seen to be anti-police, pro the criminal, always making excuses for their behaviour and suggesting reprehensible police ways.

On the other hand, being an 'insider' can help. An insider can be defined as someone who in some sense belongs to the community they are researching. They can be a geographical community, an interest community or a professional community (when research on doctors is being carried out by professionally qualified doctors, social workers by social workers, nurses by nurses, and so on). An 'outsider' can be defined as someone who exists outside that community. In my research on social work, I always make something of my being a qualified experienced social worker/senior practitioner. Although there have been some changes since I was in practice, they are not as great as some might suggest, and I am generally able – quite genuinely – to convince social workers that I know something of their real concerns. Being on duty on days when there are very many and difficult referrals, making difficult decisions about child protection, facing the competition in time between writing a court report and spending more time with the client; these are all things I have experienced, things they recognize in their own practice. It can generate a sense of trust – never entirely, I should say – arising from a realization that I have some empathy with their position. I would call it variable (different people have different perceptions) and qualified (it's not entire) trust.

Accessing areas of high sensitivity

It could be argued that all research on health and social work involves areas of high sensitivity – whether from the point of view of the sensitivity of the practitioners, the confidentiality of the information being used, or the likely evaluative outcome. This is a situation in which variable or limited access can occur, again affecting both what can be researched and the research findings.

One of the keys to this, as I have just pointed out, is the outsider/insider position. All things being equal, being an insider is liable to help in gaining access to information or sensitive aspects of sites.

An illustration of the problem of being an outsider in sensitive areas of social work is illustrated by the work of Barabara Stein described in Hammersley and Atkinson (1995). This was fieldwork carried out in several day care settings and therapeutic centres for pre-school children. The original research design – seeking to document the practice of social workers working therapeutically with children – foundered because of the problem of access.

She requested permission to observe the interaction between staff and children (with challenging behaviour) in therapeutic work. This was the first step in their attempts to correct the children's faulty emotional development. This was also the principal work of social workers at the centres. Puppet play was the key technique used by social workers, and she hoped to be able to observe them undertaking this. She was however refused access. Even after eight months' involvement and considerable negotiation, access was denied. In the end she only saw three sessions and was not allowed to take notes.

By contrast, she had assumed that data on families in the home would be out of bounds, and did not initially request access. It turned out, however, that this was not regarded as problematic by the social workers, as they viewed working with families as their 'stock in trade', and it was an area in which they themselves were interested.

Observer roles

Complete participants and complete observers

Observation is the essence of the ethnographic method. In the **complete participant** role, the researcher may join an organization or group (e.g. Alcoholics Anonymous or the staff of a mental hospital) as though he or she was an ordinary member, but with the purpose of carrying out research. This can involve deception, to the extent that they are not being truthful about the real reason for their presence. This sort of deception is needed most clearly where some brave souls are involved in research that involves a potential threat, for example with drug dealers (where it may prove inadvisable to inform the drug dealers of the real reason for your presence) (Ferrell and Hamm 1998; Weppner 1977). Complete participation may also occur where the researcher is already a member of the group and decides to carry out a study. At its extreme, total immersion in the culture is sometimes advocated, not simply 'passing yourself off' as a member, but actually becoming a member. This way you get 'inside knowledge' of perceptions and culture.

However, with complete participation, the participant has to be involved with existing expectations and routines. The researcher will therefore be hedged around by these pre-existing social routines and realities. Some fruitful lines of inquiry may be rendered impossible because they have to act in accordance with existing expectations.

The **complete observer** provides the other extreme. They have no direct contact with those they are observing (e.g. observing schoolchildren through a one-way mirror). On the positive side this can minimize the likelihood of reactivity (i.e. people reacting to the presence and purposes of the researcher and hence altering their behaviour, thus not making it 'natural'). However, there may be limits on what can and cannot be observed – indeed the complete observer role may be impossible in some settings (e.g. observing the work of a district team).

Adopting the complete participant or the complete observer role alone could make it difficult to generate accounts in a rigorous manner. It may be that some elements of each are important in carrying out ethnographic research.

Ethnographers, when dealing with areas of high sensitivity, so often characteristic of health and social work, have themselves to be aware of being sensitive and responsive to the concerns of those whom they are studying.

Listening and asking questions

Ethnography cannot be limited to merely observing what is going on in any setting. To gain any idea about the meaning of what is going on (Why are they doing this? What is their intention? What do they hope to achieve? How do they expect others to react?) one needs to ask questions of those in that setting. This does not have to take the form of formal interviews, but can be questions asked in the course of just being there, watching what's going on. Thus, one might observe in a district team a social worker getting very flustered at an apparently insignificant referral. However, we may understand this better when we know that they are on duty, that despite its insignificance they are expected to deal with it, that there are other referrals waiting to be dealt with, and that on top of this they have to write a court report. We may begin to understand how the organization of work, and the culture of the department (having to respond to need; the expectation that social workers deal with what comes in, etc.), can have a major impact on behaviour.

We cannot, in other words, understand the culture of the setting, the meaning of what people are doing, how they see their world, unless observation includes asking questions.

This can be put more formally. We can use what people say as evidence about their perspectives, and even about the larger subculture to which they belong. Knowledge of these perspectives can form an important part of the analysis, or description of the setting, group or culture. This notion of documenting perspectives, for many ethnographers, represents what ethnography is about. Thus the ethnographer does not seek (on this view) to appraise or explain the perspectives, since this might imply some superior position or knowledge on their part, or the imposition of their own cultural assumptions on another culture.

Researcher effect

If we are interested in somehow objectively presenting the accounts, perspectives and culture of groups and settings, then the question arises of the effect of the researcher on both the production of accounts and their presentation. For example, does the presence of an observer affect the ways the subjects behave? This is a serious issue because if it does, then one can seriously question the validity of findings in ethnography's own terms of reference (since the intention is to present the way things are). Interestingly, this is a similar problem presented by more positivist approaches to gaining quantitative information through surveys and experimental designs. A key issue for both is to reduce 'researcher effect' to a minimum, so as not to 'distort' the findings.

We may reasonably ask whether this is really possible, especially where it is known that the researcher is there as a researcher. It may be that as those in the setting get used to the researcher being around so their behaviour becomes increasingly normal, but, as we have seen already in the quote from the Royal Ulster Constabulary police officer (p. 165), this does not always happen. One well-known effect is the Hawthorne effect (Haralambos and Holborn 1991). This refers to a study made by researchers of factory workers. In this study they were trying to find out information about how the workers saw working in the factory. However, unexpectedly, the productivity of workers began significantly to increase (which was not an intention of the research at all). When they examined this, it became clear that this was because the workers felt more valued and committed because of the attention being paid to their views and concerns. This was a clear 'researcher effect' – an unintended consequence of researcher involvement.

Likewise, some ethnographers are unhappy with the idea of researchers openly soliciting information through planned and direct questions. This is because they might be misled by **reactivity** – the effects of the researchers on what is said. There is a danger that people respond to the researcher's agenda, rather than presenting their own perspective on the world. There is a tendency amongst some ethnographers to favour non-directive interviewing, in which the interviewee is allowed to talk at length on their own terms, as opposed to directive questioning. However, it is difficult to see how we can always get an idea of the subjective meaning of subjects' actions simply by observing, and not asking directive questions arising from, and in relation to, things that have been seen (e.g. as simple as: 'Why did you do that?').

Hammersley and Atkinson (1995) are of the view that there is no reason why the researcher should shy away from asking directive questions, particularly where this helps to embellish, or even give meaning to, data collected from observations of subjects in their setting.

Question: What is the significance for practice of understanding 'researcher effect'?

Critical appraisal

The influence of naturalism on ethnography is very great. The core of this is as follows:

- The social world should be studied in its *natural state* – i.e. as it is, rather than in some experimental design (e.g. by artificially creating comparison groups). Hence you seek to research settings 'as they are'.

- The primary aim should be to *describe* what happens in the setting.

- The research design should seek to avoid impacting on the environment (*avoid reactivity*), since this would distort the natural state and affect the validity of research findings.

- The study of the social world should be concerned with the way people understand their world (*meanings*) rather than causal laws – people do not have some mechanical relationship as with physical objects: they think, perceive and interpret the world, and act on these understandings.

Thus, the highest aim of research is to understand and present the world in the ways that subjects do, and to do so objectively.

There is a key problem here. The naturalist ethnographer seeks to *describe* and *present objectively* the way things are (people's perceptions and understandings). Hence the attempt by the ethnographer to prevent reactivity distorting findings. However, at the same time the naturalist ethnographer presents humans as constructing the social world according to their **interpretivism** – interpreting the world. The social world is no more or less than a series of interpretations by different groups. However, surely the researcher is not immune – as a human being – to this? How can they describe objectively when they too, as a human being, must be interpreting the world? An alternative is to take the view that all research is itself interpretivist. That is, the researcher is putting their own interpretation on the social world, it is just their perspective, and someone else in the same research setting might collect different data, put it together in different ways and interpret and present findings in different ways. This would especially be the case if they came from a culture different from the first researcher. However, if this were the case, the results of the research would again be no more or less than that, an interpretation, a perspective on the world. One would then have to ask: How well could such findings be used to inform policy and practice, since they would be just one view, no more or less valid than another, but certainly not some higher form of generalized knowledge with some objective status that can be applied to other settings? How can research, for example on one social or health service department, be used to inform policy on all social and health service departments, when it is just a perspective, an interpretation?

Question: What is the significance of the issue of interpretation in ethnography to the use of ethnographic findings in practice? Are there particular areas of practice for which these data are useful?

Generalizability

How far are findings from ethnography generalizable? This is an important question, for if research is to impact on policy and practice, then it needs to be seen to be relevant to settings outside the individual case that is the focus for the research. But there is no straightforward answer. Ethnographers work in detail on individual cases. Ethnographers do not seek to identify settings, necessarily because of their representativeness, and they eschew the sampling processes of survey researchers. Thus they cannot claim general applicability of findings based on representativeness. If they adopt an interpretivist position, this too undermines the possibility of generalizing. This is because, as we have seen, even the findings can only be seen as one perspective or interpretation.

Oddly, it is the idea that we can provide some description that allows us to generalize from ethnographers' case studies. This, though, is not based on sampling techniques. How can we say that findings from just a few cases or settings are of general interest?

The main way this can be achieved is by sustaining a claim that the case studied is in key ways typical of similar settings and groups. For example, if we study an acute psychiatric ward, we need to show that it is typical in important respects of all, or many, acute psychiatric wards.

Can we use this method alongside other methods?

There is no reason why not, provided you don't get into fights over the status of different forms of knowledge – positivist, interpretivist, and so on. For example, there is no reason why there could not be a complementary relationship between a wide survey research, alongside the 'in depth' ethnographic study of carefully chosen settings. This would enable the strength of ethnography – detailed rich data – to be placed alongside that of survey research, rigorously studied general findings that are representative of a particular area of social life.

Conclusion

We have now looked at two major elements of qualitative research in the human services: interviewing and ethnography. The latter's principal characteristic is observation, but includes document use and interviewing. We have seen, as with experiments, which in some respects often represent quite different intellectual traditions from ethnography and qualitative interviews, that these approaches may be subject to criticism, as well as producing applicable knowledge for practice.

Having examined approaches to data collection in qualitative methodology, it is now time to turn to its analysis. In this we examine content analysis, with particular reference to grounded theory.

Exercises

8.1 Some issues that can be discussed after reading this chapter

- What are the key characteristics of ethnography?
- What are gatekeepers? Why are they important in ethnography?
- Consider the issues raised by the question of access.
- What are 'insiders' and 'outsiders'? How can they affect findings?

- Consider the different observer roles. How can they affect research?

- What is the significance of researcher, or observer, effect?

- Consider the issue of generalizability in relation to ethnography.

8.2 An exercise using social research

Consider one of the following studies:

Murray, S. (2001) 'When a scratch becomes a 'scary story': The social construction of micro panics in centre based child care.' *Sociological Review 49*, 4, 512–529.

Wilkstrom, A. and Larson, V. (2003) 'Patient on display: A study of everyday practice in intensive care.' *Journal of Advanced Nursing 43*, 4, 376–383.

- Outline the background to the study, and the problem formulation.

- Why did the authors consider ethnography was the best way to obtain the information sought?

- Examine the methods used. What are its strengths, limitations and appropriateness for the issues addressed?

- What are the findings? Are there gaps?

- What are the conclusions to the study? Are they justified by the evidence? Do the authors identify the limits to the study?

- How can this study be applied to practice? How useful is it? Which ways might it be used? What are its limitations in this respect?

Examples of ethnographic research

Floersch, J. (2000) 'Reading the case record: The oral and written narratives of social workers.' *Social Services Review 74*, 2, 169–192.

Griffiths, J. (1998) 'Meeting personal hygiene needs in the community: A district nursing perspective on the health and social care divide.' *Health and Social Care in the Community 6*, 234–240.

Macleod, M. (1994) 'It's the little things that count: The hidden complexity of everyday clinical nursing practice.' *Journal of Clinical Nursing 3*, 6, 361–368.

Mamas, E. and Street, A. (2000) 'The handover: Uncovering the hidden practices of nurses.' *International Journal of Critical Care Nursing 16*, 6, 373–383.

Martinez, B. (1986) 'Community oriented social work in a rural and remote Hebridean patch.' *International Social Work 29*, 349–372.

Pithouse, A. (1998) *Social Work: The Social Organisation of an Invisible Trade.* Aldershot: Ashgate.

Scott, D. (1997) 'Inter agency conflict: An ethnographic study.' *Child and Family Social Work 2*, 73–80.

Wakefield, A. (1999) 'Clinical practice: Changes that occur in nursing when a patient is categorised as terminally ill.' *International Journal of Palliative Nursing 5*, 4, 171–176.

Wilkstrom, A. and Larson, V. (2003) 'Patient on display: A study of everyday practice in intensive care.' *Journal of Advanced Nursing 43*, 4, 376–383.

Further reading

Bakeman, R. and Gottman, J. (1997) *Observing Interaction.* Cambridge: Cambridge University Press.

Berg, B. (2001) *Qualitative Research Methodology.* Boston, MA: Allyn and Bacon.

Groenkjar, M. (2002) 'Critical ethnographic methodology in nursing research: Issues and solutions.' *Contemporary Nurse 14*, 1, 49–55.

Hammersley, M. (1992) *Reading Ethnographic Research.* London: Routledge.

Hammersley, M. (1992) *What's Wrong with Ethnography?* London: Routledge.

Hammersley, M. and Atkinson, P. (1995) *Ethnography: Principles in Practice.* London: Routledge.

Sands, R.G. (1990) 'Ethnographic research: A qualitative research approach to the study of the interdisciplinary team.' *Social Work in Health Care 15*, 115–129.

CHAPTER NINE

Content Analysis – Grounded Theory

When you have carried out interviews, observed situations (and taken notes) or collected documents, you simply have just that – a range of documents recording conversations, observations or information. They are, on the surface, very different from each other (individually), and you are in a position in which you simply have 'raw data'.

What they have in common, however, is their focus, broadly, on the same subject area (e.g. reasons why young people offend, experience of older people of residential care or the process of admission to psychiatric hospital). Thus, they are both as different as the different accounts contained within them, and similar in that those accounts cover the same broad areas.

How do you put this together in a way that enables you to draw conclusions or make observations on the whole area for study – the topic you are interested in? To do this you need to draw out themes that emerge from the data. What this involves is identifying common domains, topics, issues, and so on, that occur in the different accounts, from which you will be able to comment on their place in your study. For example, if you are looking at reasons why young people offend, you might find themes of boredom ('there's nothing else to do in this place'), of excitement ('it gives me a kick to run the risk of getting caught') or poverty ('how else am I going to get those trainers?'). If you were looking at the experience of admission to psychiatric hospital, you might find themes of stigma (a sense of shame at being admitted), consternation (a worry about what might happen) or relief ('at last I have sought help').

This approach is called content analysis – it is where you analyse the primary source material for common contents that enable you to make general comments on the topic of study.

It is **reductionist** – that is, it seeks to 'reduce' the complicated mass of individualized data into areas or themes common to much of the group. The themes that emerge will not always fit the whole group. For example, some adolescents may say that they steal because it gives them a kick of excitement, while others may refer to poverty. There may be a crossover – getting a kick and responding to poverty may be responses that sometimes go together. What we are doing when we conduct content analysis is making a judgement about key themes that emerge from the data, and writing about them as common characteristics in that particular group.

Grounded theory

An inductive approach

Grounded theory (GT) is perhaps the most widely used form of content analysis. What is GT? According to Glaser and Strauss (1968), who developed it (see also Strauss and Corbin 1998), GT is theory that is derived from data systematically gathered and analysed through the research process. What does this mean?

This is what is called an *inductive* approach, which may be contrasted with the *deductive* approach that characterizes more quantitative contents. You will remember from earlier chapters that in a deductive approach you identify a hypothesis or proposition, which you then seek to test by setting up research to examine whether that proposition is true or false. For example, you may make the proposition: Women with traditional sex-role orientations are more likely to find caring for their children at home a rewarding activity than women without traditional sex-role orientations. You would then set up a research project which would enable you to focus on women caring for children at home, from which you can distinguish those with traditional sex-role orientations and those without such orientations, and then focus on how they feel about caring for their children. The result might serve to confirm or falsify your overall proposition.

According to GT this could turn out to be something like trying to fit square pegs into round holes. How do you know, for example, that the issue of sex-role orientation is one that exercises these women at all? Even if it does, it may not be an important issue for them. By focusing on this issue, you force them to reply in relation to issues defined in advance by the researcher, issues which may not be of particular importance in the women's lived lives. It may be the case that there is found to be a relationship between satisfaction with the child care role and sex-role orientation, but the die-hard GT researcher could well say: So what? How do we know that this issue is of any particular significance in the women's lived lives? Maybe it wouldn't even come into their consciousness if they were not asked in the first place.

An inductive approach does not start with a proposition about the (social) world. The researcher does not begin the research with a preconceived theory or proposition in mind. Rather the researcher begins with an area of study, and allows the theory or themes to emerge from the data. Thus, we might start with a general question: How do women feel about caring for their children at home where they do not have outside paid employment? No assumptions are made about any kind of relationships (between, for example, attitudes to sex roles and satisfaction with the child care role). Indeed, no assumption is made about the significance of sex-role orientation in the first place.

Theory derived from the data (that is, the information gathered through, for example, interviews and observation) is, according to GT, more likely to resemble the 'reality' than is theory derived from putting together a series of concepts (such as sex-role orientation) based only on experience or speculation. This is what is meant by 'grounding' theory – what you are doing is grounding your theory on the data, or more generally, and through the data, the lived experiences and accounts of the subjects of study. Thus, you are in that respect much more closely going to resemble the lived reality of the subjects than the use of speculative hypotheses, which seals off as much as it introduces by making too precise a focus at the outset.

The issue of themes emerged in research I undertook on mental health professionals in both health and social work arenas (Sheppard 1991). In this, I was looking at some of the key features that characterized brief intervention, in particular those most valued by clients or service users. It became clear that, in a brief context, it was the relationship qualities of the practitioner (what they were like), rather than their expert skills (what they could do) that were most important. Thus the key qualities identified were the capacity to listen, the care and commitment of the practitioner, and empathy and understanding. This compared with extended intervention, where information, advice, the capacity to analyse the situation and to increase self-understanding played a more prominent part. All of these constitute themes that became apparent from an examination of the range of cases.

> Grounded theory is grounded in the sense that it develops themes from the data collected, the lived lives of individuals.

Verstehen

Grounded theory seeks to achieve a subjective understanding of the lived world of the subjects of study. In this respect the researcher's task is one of involvement and understanding. What is this about? Well, one way of looking at the research process is to view the researcher as a detached observer. Detached observers seek to examine the social situation without themselves being involved, and being as objective as possible in analysing and presenting findings. However, GT does not see the role of the investigator as being that of the detached observer, whose task is to describe social behaviour in terms of causal forces external to the individual (e.g. the 'cause' of juvenile delinquency is poverty and disadvantage).

GT emphasizes the more involved role of the social researcher. This is a humanistic vision of social science, where a verstehen approach requires that the researcher should seek an empathic understanding of the people they are studying. Thus, if, for example, you are studying women in the middle years who have suffered bereavement, you will seek to make sense of their responses by putting yourself in their shoes. What would it be like to be in this position? When they say they are embarrassed by friends trying to arrange convenient blind dates with middle-aged men, you look carefully at the data, and try to imagine what it would be like to be in this position, and think about the feelings you might have. In doing this, you are using your essential humanity (that you can have feelings of frustration, embarrassment, stupidity, and so on) to enable you to understand what it is that the respondents are saying in their accounts.

This requires the social researcher, in the technical terminology, to pay attention to the 'social meanings' used by participants, whose actions are predicated on the way they understand their situations. The first task of the social researcher is to describe how the actors themselves act towards their world on the basis of *how they see it*, rather than how it appears to outside observers.

Question: How can research employing verstehen as a central approach inform you in relation to practice?

Theory in the research process

At the heart of the research process is the attempt to create concepts that help to explain what is going on in any subject area of research. Part of this involves **conceptual ordering**. This refers to the organization of data into discrete categories according to their characteristics (more properly their properties and dimensions) and then using description to expand upon and elucidate these categories. We may, for example, be distinguishing between types of parents. We may identify different groups: authoritarian parents, sensitive parents, inconsistent/unpredictable parents. I have simplified key findings in child development here, for the purpose of clarity and illustration (see Baumrind 1971; Maccoby and Martin 1983):

- *Authoritarian parents* would, for example, have the characteristic of being very disciplinarian, always determined to keep a low threshold before setting strong boundaries, and showing little tendency to respond to, or even encourage the children to tell them, their concerns.

- *Sensitive parents* might be characterized by a strong tendency to responsiveness to the child's concerns. They will want to hear the child's story before deciding whether to respond with discipline or sympathy, and will be aware that children sometimes behave badly because they are upset rather than bad.

- *Inconsistent/unpredictable* parents could veer between the two above approaches. At times they may be short with the child, not interested in their explanations, and emphasize the setting of boundaries; at others they will be more responsive and wish to hear the child's story before making decisions. It may be difficult for the child to know 'which parent' they will be confronting.

What the categories do is enable the researcher (a) to identify common types of objects, attitudes, situations and (b) to distinguish between one common class of object and another. Thus we would be able to identify parents who had common characteristics of being, for example, authoritarian, and at the same time distinguish them from those who were sensitive or inconsistent. We do this, in the first instance, by identifying the range of characteristics that exist in parents. For example, we could look at (a) boundary setting, (b) the extent to which parents delay decision making, (c) preparedness to listen to the child, and (d) consistency of actions between one incident and another. We would be able to identify dimensions across these categories. For example, in relation to boundary setting we might identify those with rigid and strong boundaries, and others with more flexible and perhaps less harsh boundaries. It is through these dimensions that we can begin to classify the key categories that will enable us to conduct content analysis, identifying the 'types' of parents in our study. Putting them together enables us to construct typologies of parents.

Conceptual ordering allows us to order the concepts in terms of a hierarchy of explanatory power. Thus we can distinguish classes and categories. For example, a *class* of object could be furniture; *categories* of objects within that class of objects would be tables, chairs, wardrobes, bookshelves, and so on. The higher order concept is that of furniture, and we have described the categories of objects that comprise that class of object.

The conceptual ordering in our example of parents would, for example, enable us to look at:

- a class – parent
- categories – authoritarian, sensitive, and inconsistent.

Typically, conceptual ordering can, for example, seek to depict the class of perspective or action carried out by people who are the subject of the study in relation to the focus of the study (in this case the focus of the study might be different types of parenting manifested by parents with young children).

> Themes developed through content analysis and grounded theory are designed to develop concepts and theories that pay due attention to meanings.

Question: What part can concepts play in the conduct of practice?

WHAT IS THEORY?

For grounded theorists, 'theory' denotes a set of well developed categories/themes/concepts that are systematically interrelated through statements of relationship to enable them to form a theoretical framework that explains some relevant social, psychological or educational etc. phenomenon'. This is a mouthful, so we should explore what this means.

The statement of relationship explains who, what, where, when, why and with what consequences things occur.

Let us take again the example of parenting. We would seek not just to identify and conceptually classify what the different types of parent are (which according to GT we should not assume in advance), but we would also wish to explain why it is that they might behave in this way. We might, for example, have further categories that relate to a sense of the 'controllability' of the child, or to personal competence in the parent. It may be that we then relate these two factors to parenting style to begin to bring out a statement of relationship between the different concepts and categories. Without labouring the definition of our new categories too much, we might find the relationships occur along the following lines:

- Authoritarian parents: tend to be parents who have a low sense of personal competence, and feel that the child could easily become uncontrollable.

- Sensitive parents may be parents who have a high sense of personal competence, and feel able to control the child regardless of how they behave.

- Inconsistent parents may be those who have a feeling that they can control certain kinds of situation but not others – hence they do not respond in a consistent manner.

Thus we have theoretical statements of relationships that help us to understand the ways in which parents behave towards young children.

It should be said that many people do not regard the interrelationships of concepts to be the most significant thing, and rather feel that the generation of concepts (such as those on parenting) are sufficient.

Flexibility and the research question

The relationship between the research question and data collection in grounded theory is one characterized, as in all aspects, by flexibility.

Just as researchers have to be aware of emergent themes within the data to create concepts and theories, so they must recognize that framing a research question too rigidly can close off options for learning and developing ideas from the data. The key thing is to frame the research question in a way that gives the freedom to explore a phenomenon in depth.

Thus what we do is seek to start off with an initial broad question that becomes progressively narrowed and more focused as the research process proceeds. The question needs:

- to be open and broad
- to identify the phenomena to be studied
- to tell the reader what the researcher wants to know about the subject.

For example, we may address the question: How do women manage pregnancy complicated by illness? This is clearly about (a) pregnancy and (b) complications. But it also looks at the management of the pregnancy from the woman's perspective. It does not specify in any detail the relationship between elements which cannot be determined in advance (e.g. including women's health beliefs, doctors' actions, availability and type of support, etc.).

Flexibility can also mean *changing the focus of the question*. A researcher might enter the field having a general notion about what they might want to study. If they are carefully listening to, or observing, the speech and actions of respondents, then analysis should lead them to discover the issues that are important or problematic in respondents' lives. Paying attention to respondents' concerns is where the focus of a research project should be.

An example, not of a general question, but of a key aspect of research, comes from my work on social work practice with depressed mothers in child and family care (Sheppard 2001), in which I was interested in discovering (first of all) how accurately social workers identified the presence of depression. I reasoned that their capacity to do so was likely to be crucial in determining their practice strategies. I developed a way of assessing the presence of depression and of assessing the social workers' own assessments. However, on examination of the transcripts, this was not the key way they considered the women at all. They were more concerned with making what I called 'moral predictive judgements'. These were judgements about the woman's personality and behaviour that contained within them an element that would help give some guidance of the likely risk to the child. Hence it was not the depression itself that was important, but the way in which the depression was incorporated into the woman's personality and actions to make risk more or less likely. Thus we distinguished between stoical women who coped in adversity, from the genuinely depressed, who nevertheless were able to be aware of the importance of the child's needs, to the 'troubled and troublesome', who were more chaotic and less able and willing to focus on the child's needs.

> A key element in the development of concepts and themes, indeed in the conduct of the research itself, is the flexibility of the researcher and their capacity to respond to the data they are collecting and use it to develop their ideas.

Using the case to learn – The process of building grounded theory
In this methodology data collection and analysis are meant to occur in alternating sequences. Analysis begins with the first interview and observations, and leads to the next interview and observations, followed

by more analysis, interviews, and so on. It is the analysis that derives from data collection, but also the data collection (we shall see) that derives from the analysis.

At the heart of this process is the verstehen mentioned earlier. This also entails a focus, however, on the accounts of the respondents. It is generally considered to involve a willingness to listen and 'give voice' to respondents – hearing what others have to say, seeing what others do, and representing them as accurately as possible. Hence a key purpose of GT is the *most accurate representation possible of the meanings attached by respondents* to facets of the particular issue with which we are concerned (as researcher).

The GT way of theory building is not to treat cases individually, one after another, simply identifying themes that emerge (although a concern with themes is a central issue). Rather researchers want to know what this case (e.g. an interview with a particular woman about ill health during pregnancy) teaches us about other cases. We want to move from the specific (the individual case) to the more general (the area as a whole). Thus we use a case to open up our minds about the range of possibilities, meanings and themes that may exist in the data. When we move on to the next case, we will be more sensitive to the possibilities that themes exist, as well as what else a case might teach us.

For example, we may find that when researching health complications in pregnancy, our first interview does show up a number of facets to be important to the (individual) woman interviewed. This may be, for example, the sensitivity of the doctor, the response of the mother, the seriousness and 'fear factor' in the illness, the stage of pregnancy, and so on. These then become issues that can be borne in mind when looking at the next case – Is the doctor's sensitivity an issue in this case also? What about the mother – was she around and important?

But other facets might emerge: in the second case the woman might start talking about the proximity of the hospital or the availability of her husband. Here we are aware that there are some case-based differences, and new (possible) themes emerge. In looking at the next case we might seek those out, and as we accrue cases, we can begin to judge the extent to which these are general themes, and the extent to which they are just facets of individual cases.

Question: Are there aspects of grounded theory, particularly that of building theory, that have relevance for the work of the practitioner? Are there elements in the practice of the researcher that may be mirrored in the practice of the practitioner? Does it, for example, provide ideas for the development of 'practice wisdom'?

Theoretical sampling

Closely related to theory building is the process of theoretical sampling. Here, the questions are: How should we proceed in conducting the research? What is the relationship between our provisional findings (based on a few cases) and the process by which we try to get further information through, say, interviews? Who should we be interviewing?

Theoretical sampling is the preferred option where we do not wish to predetermine the study sample before the research (as for example when we seek to get a 'representative' sample of a particular group, such as pregnant mothers). It is based on concepts that emerge in the data in analysis, and that appear to have particular relevance to the topic. What we seek to do is sample those settings or individuals that will maximize our opportunity to focus on particular themes emerging from the data.

For example, if a researcher were studying the care of patients in mental hospital, and the concept of 'work flow' became a major category, varying by ward, time (day/night, etc.), the researcher might decide to focus on all three shifts (having previously only looked at one), as well as different types of hospital wards. What they are doing is choosing a sample that will enable them to focus more effectively on important emergent themes.

Now, if the concept of 'work flow' is important, we can ask ourselves: How did the staff organize themselves? What part did the patients play? What were the obstacles and enhancing factors to work flow? How did management/instruction/expectations affect work flow?

CODING

Coding is the means by which we are actually able to themetisize the data. Coding is the means by which we identify the emergent themes from the data. GT starts off by a process of **open coding**. The central purpose of this is to open the inquiry widely. What we are seeking to do here is tentatively identify a large number of potential themes from the data. We are, at this point, naming and labelling a large range of possible concepts. As matters go on, so you may be able to find groups of concepts that come together and form a category. This process begins to whittle down the number of themes emergent from the data. It is a process of reduction to help clarity, understanding and explanation.

Axial coding builds on open coding, bringing together those lower level themes or concepts into higher order themes or concepts. Suppose we are looking at drug use by adolescents. We may have a number of phrases used to denote this: 'trying just a few' or 'being careful about what drug is being used', or 'using less potent drugs'. Our translation of this might be into a general term called 'limited experimenting'.

Selective coding is the process of integrating and refining these categories as the basis for a developing theory. An example of this is in the point above (p.183) about different types of parenting. Researchers are constantly comparing the products of their analysis against the actual data emerging in the new cases which they are studying – the **comparative method**. As this process occurs, so they can make modifications, and adjust their definitions (for example) of the themes and categories that are emerging to take account of new information provided by the new cases.

We can also use comparison of terms used in our data with the way it is used in other contexts to sensitize us to its meaning. For example, a residential worker, or staff nurse, may state that they would rather work with an experienced colleague during the night, rather than a student or other inexperienced worker, because 'I end up doing all the work'. To gain some understanding of the significance of the term 'experience', we can compare it with its use in other contexts. For example, an inexperienced driver would tend to be more cautious, slower, prone to make mistakes, unsure of themselves, reluctant to take the initiative, and so on. These may be of considerable relevance to the practitioner working at night.

Theoretical saturation denotes that during the analysis no new properties and dimensions emerge from the data when we look at succeeding cases, and that we are, therefore, learning nothing new from the new cases. They simply serve to confirm facets and themes already developed.

Critical appraisal

Dealing with the close up – micro

The grounded theory approach tends to encourage the researcher to focus on the 'close up' features of social interaction – the immediate aspects of individuals' lived lives – like the experience of pregnancy, or of being a mental patient, or of parenting difficult children. However, this neglects the seemingly more remote aspects of setting and context. For example, it is important to understand that forms of behaviour cannot be understood simply in terms of the mixture of personalities involved or the dynamics of the particular situation (e.g. between the parent and child in parenting). The wider work setting, economics and culture play important parts. For example, we may need to pay attention to the processes giving rise to cultural expectations that women are to be primary carers for their children. It may be this, for example, that is responsible for some women feeling under so much pressure that they are more authoritarian or find reacting sensitively and responsively to a child more difficult.

One of the key points is that those values and expectations representing group norms become part of the structure of society. These facets exert constraints and influences – perhaps in different ways – on all women who are parents, and may therefore be considered to have some kind of causal relationship to the conduct of parenting. Indeed, this may be underlined by social policy decisions that, for example, emphasize the importance of the family and women's part in it, rather than their role as employees and workers. This may serve to reinforce cultural expectations, which, if they do not become a 'straitjacket', may certainly circumscribe women's opportunities as parents.

Dealing with the far off – macro

Power is not a subject greatly discussed in the context of GT. In GT – if it is pinned down – power is a notion that is confined to a situation involving a relationship between two or more people in which control is exercised by at least one of them over others. A paradigm of this would be an armed robber going to a bank, threatening the bank clerk, getting the money and getting away. But this ignores other sources and locations of power, which in practical terms could be more significant. In particular we are directed away from collective power sources (money, information, property, force of law, etc.). Such conditions of power are embodied in business and systems of stratification of all kinds – the 'macro' level of society.

If, for example, we look at my study with depressed mothers (Sheppard 2001) we were confronted by social workers who quite generally were not responding to the needs of the mother as an individual in her own right, rather as a parent. This could have been explained at the level of individual expectations and interaction, but I did not think that adequate. To understand this we needed to examine the structural-cultural environment that strongly influenced social workers to direct them away from responding to the women's personal needs. Thus we got a cultural manifestation of 'I am the social worker for the child' (and hence not the mother). But behind this lay an interpretation of legislation that 'the welfare of the child is paramount'. Likewise, many child protection inquiries had emphasized the conflict of interest between parent and child and the dangers of making mistakes responding to parental rather than child need. However, this imported an implicit conflict of interest thesis between mother and child that was frequently inappropriate to a situation where the mother genuinely cared for the child, but was struggling in adverse circumstances.

Thus we had (a) *departmental directives* and (b) *law* – which was interpreted in particular ways (hence social policy) – providing 'power points' that operated in effect at the level of structure impacting on the individual practices of the social workers, and most definitely on the experiences of the women. This was backed up by a structure of authority, which in social services departments, involved tiers of management. The manager's task is, in part, to keep the social workers on line, to ensure policies and procedures are followed. Thus we have an emergent culture leading to neglect of the women's needs, and a structure, with power points, to ensure this is maintained.

To take all this into account involves focusing on the 'macro' level of society, rather than the 'micro' level of individual interactions. GT is far better attuned to dealing with the latter rather than the former.

Linking subjective and objective

Grounded theory is a very subjectivist approach to knowledge development. Although grounded theorists talk of the 'discovery' of GT, and hence imply some sort of objective status, the approach made by GT concentrates on invoking the subjective world of respondents, and then developing themes and theories from this, through which we can understand the lived lives of the groups in relation to our research area.

However, grounded theorists do not seek to create a convergence between their humanist/subjective approach and more scientific objectivist research and theory. We look at aspects of social structure that exist objectively and in some respects independently of the people we are studying, but it is perfectly possible to view such aspects as providing a 'frame' through which we are able to understand individual actions and social relations. For example, a society characterized by a non-sex-role stereotype set of norms would exert a clear impact in the range of possibilities open to a mother, when compared with one characterized by traditional sex-role stereotypes. Likewise, the institution of the family might work in a way that enabled women to limit their child care responsibilities. Both these would be objective elements of the social structure heavily influencing social action and interaction.

Observable and non-observable

Grounded theory is limited by insisting that its concepts exclusively emerge from the observed data of research – that they should directly represent the perspectives and behaviour of the people being studied. Such a focus cannot tell us about the mechanisms that may exist beyond the observable 'surface' and contribute to the formation of observable features.

Conclusion

As with the qualitative interview (Chapter Seven) and ethnography (Chapter Eight) we are again confronted with processes that may be subject to critical appraisal. It becomes apparent that, like the quantitative approaches we have looked at (surveys and experimental designs), these more qualitative approaches are subject to certain criticisms, based on their approaches and limitations. It is important to remember that this is generally the case for different methodologies. It is significant, therefore, to be aware both of the strengths and limitations of certain approaches on the one hand, and how different approaches may be valuable in different ways for practice. We may, for example, be able to obtain certain kinds of information from qualitative interviews (such as the experiences of intervention) and other kinds of information from other approaches (experimental designs may be more appropriate for measuring change and outcome).

Evaluation, too, is not just a matter for quantitative research. Qualitative methods may be used also to evaluate programmes and interventions, and it is to this that we now turn.

Exercises

9.1 Some issues that can be discussed after reading this chapter

- What is the importance of themes?

- What is verstehen? Consider its significance for research and practice.

- What is conceptual ordering? Distinguish concepts and theories.

- What is the significance of flexibility?

- Discuss the process of theory building. What part does coding play?

9.2 An exercise using an article employing content analysis

Consider one of the following:

Holland, S. (2000) 'The assessment relationship: Interactions between social workers and parents in the child protection process.' *British Journal of Social Work 30*, 2, 149–165.

Magnusson, A., Severinsson, E. and Lutzen, K. (2003) 'Reconstructing mental health nursing in home care.' *Journal of Advanced Nursing 43*, 4, 351–359.

- Briefly outline the aims and objectives of the paper.

- How well does the paper follow expectations of the method used (content analysis)?

- Place the methods outlined, within the wider context of content analysis, as a method.
- Consider the findings and their use for practice.
- Critically appraise the use of content analysis as a method of social research.

Examples of research employing content analysis

Holland, S. (2000) 'The assessment relationship interactions between social workers and parents in the child protection process.' *British Journal of Social Work 30*, 2, 149–165.

Magnusson, A., Severinsson, E. and Lutzen, K. (2003) 'Reconstructing mental health nursing in home care.' *Journal of Advanced Nursing 43*, 4, 351–359.

O'Callaghan, C. (2001) 'Bringing music to life: A study of music therapy and palliative care experiences in a cancer hospital.' *Journal of Palliative Care 17*, 3, 155–160.

Sheppard, M., Newstead, S., DiCaccavo, A. and Ryan, K. (2000) 'Reflexivity and the development of process knowledge in social work: A classification and empirical study.' *British Journal of Social Work 30*, 465–488.

Somerset, M., Faulkner, A., Shaw, A., Dunn, L. and Sharp, D. (1999) 'Obstacles in the path to a primary care led national health service: Complexities of outpatient care.' *Social Science and Medicine 48*, 2, 213–225.

Woodcock, J. (2003) 'The social work assessment of parenting: An exploration.' *British Journal of Social Work 33*, 87–106.

Wright, F. (2000) 'The role of family care givers for an older person resident in a care home.' *British Journal of Social Work 30*, 649–661.

Zhang, A. and Siminoff, L. (2003) 'The role of the family in treatment decisions making by patients with cancer.' *Oncology Nursing Forum 30*, 6, 1022–1028.

Further reading

Berg, B.L. (2001) *Qualitative Research Methods for the Social Sciences*. Boston, MA: Allyn and Bacon.

Layder, D. (1993) *New Strategies in Social Research*. London: Polity Press.

Miles, M. and Huberman, A. (1994) *Qualitative Data Analysis*. London: Sage.

Strauss, A. and Corbin, J. (1998) *Basics of Qualitative Research*. Thousand Oaks, CA: Sage.

CHAPTER TEN
Qualitative Evaluation

Qualitative research may seek to create descriptions, seek interpretations (of participants) or find explanations of facets of the social world related to social work. It does so, on the whole, through interviewing and observing people (although documentation may also be used).

So, where we are looking at young offending, for example, we may seek to find their reasons for being involved with gangs or with car thefts or with joy riding. They may explain that it is all about the excitement they get, or because 'all their mates do it', or because they don't see why they shouldn't have what they want – they're 'pissed off' with rich kids getting all the good stuff and they want designer track suits and the like.

Likewise, when we look at health or social work, we may seek to identify what are the main ways of relating to residents in an old people's home, how they developed, and the reasons for behaving in this way. This way we get a picture of the workings of the home, and what may be expected. Where it is typical of many others, it may give us an idea of old people's homes in general. The same questions may arise in relation to nurse practice in a psychiatric ward, or in relation to our wish to understand health visitor perceptions of the social dynamics between them and mothers of children aged under one.

However, in health and social work we are not just interested in description, interpretation and explanation. We are interested in evaluation. Evaluation can focus on as many activities as those in which social or health workers are involved. How effective, for example, is task-centred practice with agoraphobic people? How far is a parenting skills programme able to respond to the needs of parents whose children are on the child protection register? What qualities in nurses do relatives of cancer victims value most highly? How can we most effectively encourage partnership with parents and children in need? And so on.

The point about evaluation is that the term *value* is at its heart. We seek to place a value on one or other particular form of intervention. Is one form of intervention more effective in reaching certain goals than another? Do people experience certain qualities in a health or social worker to be of particular significance in the conduct of practice? To what extent do service users, patients or clients feel satisfied with the service they receive? In each case, people are asked to put a value on what it is that is being undertaken in intervention.

In general, two forms of evaluation are distinguished:

- outcome evaluation
- process evaluation.

Outcome evaluation assesses the effects produced by policies, programmes and practices, and the extent to which such results measure up to programme goals. Suppose, for example, we have a goal of reducing rates of re-offending in clients of the youth offenders team. We might try some innovative practice, designed to raise their self-esteem (e.g. involvement with an educational scheme, or with an apprenticeship scheme). We could then focus on this group and see if their re-offending rates went down. We could do this better still by comparing with another group who did not have this intervention, and so on.

Process evaluation seeks to identify what seem to be the most important elements in the conduct of any given programme, and to discover the ways these relate to each other within the programme. One feature in this might be the client's experience of health or social worker intervention. How far did the client experience the practitioner as understanding, or sympathetic, empathic, or insightful into their situation? How responsive were they to their stated needs? We may, further-more, seek to relate process to outcome: What were the most important elements contributing to the outcome of any given programme or work (e.g. more speedy removal from the child protection register; quicker response rates in accident and emergency)?

In short, outcome evaluation focuses on the nature, degree and, to some extent, the cause of any changes that occur; process evaluation focuses on what actually happens in the processes involved in intervention.

There has been a tendency (e.g. Cheetham *et al.* 1992) to associate process evaluation with the so-called soft methodologies of qualitative research, and outcome evaluation with the so-called hard methodologies of quantitative research, particularly experimental design. In truth, both methods can be used for both areas, although they would look, to say the least, rather different.

Although, inevitably, policy makers are often very concerned with outcomes (Does this practice, policy, programme or piece of legislation work?), process evaluation is very important also. We can get an idea not only of the complex processes by which intervention takes place, but also of the rationale for it, according to practitioners. This is particularly so in service-user research, where we are expected to value the service user, respect them as persons, or even empower them! If this is so, then issues like the manner through which health and social workers relate to clients, and their experience of the process of intervention generally, are very important. We evaluate processes that we regard as valuable. The manner and means of service provision is important, perhaps regardless of outcome. We might (as with Corney 1984) find that social work in-tervention makes very little difference in terms of *outcome* for depressed women in general practice settings, but we may find that *the women them-selves regarded the social work help very highly*, and that they were glad they received this help.

However, there is no reason that outcomes cannot be rated qualita-tively (in principle). Many of those of a quantitative, particularly experimental, disposition would dismiss ideas that this could be the case, but, using interpretivist qualitative methodologies, we can explore with the client those facets they regarded as important (rather than those imposed by service providers or legislators), and we can gain their perspective on how they had affected them, in their terms of reference. This would most certainly be considered 'soft' research by some, but it is entirely consistent with ideas of those who see obtaining the subjective perceptions of those being researched as the prime purpose of research.

What kinds of studies are associated with qualitative evaluations?

Qualitative evaluations are often associated with interpretivist perspectives (although they do not have to be). What does this mean? It means that in carrying out evaluations, we are interested in people's interpretations, or perspectives, on what is going on, and how this is affecting them. Evaluation involves measuring matters in terms of those interpretations and perspectives. How we evaluate a programme or intervention is in terms of interpretations of process or of outcome. Where we look at more than one group (for example service users, practitioners and managers) we evaluate matters in terms of multiple interpretations. And these reflect how they view matters. We can look at this **interpretivist evaluation** in two ways.

First, we can view it in terms of the goals set by legislators, agencies or researchers. What are the service users' experience of intervention? How do they tally with the intentions of the agencies, legislators or policy makers? One example of this sort of thing could be to look at the quality of partnership between social workers and parents in child protection. This is an issue that the Department of Health has 'banged on' about for years, even having the dubiously titled book *The Challenge of Partnership in Child Protection* (Department of Health 1995). We could look at the service users' experience of intervention in terms of key aspects of partnership: How involved were they in discussion about what intervention should take place? What part did they play in case confer-ences? How involved were they in carrying out the decisions of case conferences (participation in doing the problem-resolving work, etc.)? These are issues, with a focus on maternal depression, that I looked at in my study with depressed mothers (Sheppard 2001).

Second, we could, alternatively, emphasize the themes and issues that emerge from the participants themselves. Thus, when we try to eval-uate research, it is not so much in terms of goals set by agencies, legisla-tors or researchers, but in terms of the issues that are important to the participants (e.g. the practitioners or service users). Thus we could carry out open-ended semi-structured interviews that focus on questions like: What happened when the health or social workers came to see you? What were the important facets of what the practitioner did? Were there any facets you were pleased about? Were there aspects you were less pleased about? Now, here we would look to issues that emerged. For ex-ample, a theme that might emerge in relation to one or more of the ques-tions might be the friendliness or approachability of the practitioner, or the lack of it. As a result of carrying out open-ended interviews, we would begin to get at themes and issues that were the concern of the ser-vice users' in the service users' own terms of reference (not ours, or those of legislators or agencies) (Fisher 1983; Fisher, Marsh and Philips 1986).

In the first case, we are interested in service users' views of the agen-das set by others (legislators, agencies, etc.). In the second case, we are interested in how the service users perceive their world, how they 'con-struct' what is going on. It does strongly suggest, in this latter case, that:

- the way we (e.g. as legislators) see the world is profoundly different from the way they (e.g. as clients) see it

- potentially the clients see it very differently

- in such complex situations it is better to seek clients' perspectives of interventions than to view our starting assumptions to be the best way to view the programme or intervention.

This kind of qualitative evaluation allows you to understand and capture the nature and range of perspectives of participants (whoever they are) without predetermining the range of perspectives available through prior selection of questionnaire categories.

> Qualitative evaluation is concerned with value (in its general sense) and seeks to use qualitative methods to enable us to assign particular value to different forms of health or social work activity.

Studies of service users: Client-perspective studies

We frequently nowadays come across client-perspective or service-user studies. It seems that no evaluation is complete without this. It focuses on their experiences of, or evaluations about, particular interventions. And this is often used to influence policy and practice. Many of the early studies argued that a concern with user perspectives reflects an interest in the individual's subjective experience, that what is important is not some clinical and so-called objective outcome measure but the lived experiences of the people who are being researched.

This comes from a very different tradition from outcome studies that seek to place some objectivity on matters. For example, does it matter if, in a study of psychiatric nurse or social work intervention with depressed women, the women like the practitioner, feel valued and empathized with, if all their efforts make no difference to outcome? That is, would the women remain as depressed as they would have been if they had had no intervention? That would be the view of the more objectivist evaluator, often employing quantitative methods. The goal, according to them, is to reduce the presence and severity of depression, and that is what is important.

Those of a more interpretivist disposition would say that it is not our part to decide what is the appropriate goal, and that the service users should give their evaluation in their own terms. Thus, if (a) they value friendliness, openness and empathy and (b) the practitioner shows this, that is enough, regardless of whether or not the depression has been lifted. One might argue, from the service users' point of view, that the real issue is their capacity to negotiate the depression without feeling so personally isolated (rather than the cure of the depression) and this is what the social workers achieved in general practice settings (see Corney 1984). Using these methods gives a closer approximation to the understanding and perceptions of those at the receiving end.

Nowadays, there is often a more eclectic approach to service-user research. There is often a combination of quantitative and qualitative measures (e.g. rating the degree of satisfaction alongside more qualitative questions on experience of intervention). This is not just about eclecticism, there are also pragmatic considerations. The conduct and analysis of semi-structured interviews can be an exhausting, and costly, process. To stick rigidly to qualitative techniques can considerably reduce the areas that can be exposed to comment and evaluation. Nevertheless, the interpretivist tradition remains very strong.

Pluralist or multiple-perspective evaluation

Pluralist evaluation involves getting multiple perspectives on processes and outcomes of interventions. The emphasis on getting the perspectives of participants is again consistent with the interpretivist tradition. It is also about the nature of health and social work. For example, many believe that social work is a messy business, with far too many factors or variables present to be able to conduct simple, elegant controlled trials or experiments. Furthermore, whose perspective are we taking when we claim to be obtaining some objective results? For these people, a key element in evaluation is getting multiple perspectives, and seeing how they relate to each other. Why is this?

- Ambiguity and diversity rather than clarity of goals is the
  norm for social welfare organizations.

- The distinction between means (social work processes) and ends (outcomes of intervention) is an artificial and shifting one.

- Most importantly, traditional evaluation demands an assumption of consensus and unity amongst all parties, in which the criteria for success can be defined and the extent to which they are attained measured (e.g. to reduce re-offending amongst young offenders). Whereas pluralistic evaluation recognizes consensus is absent (reducing offending may not be the goal of the young offender themselves) and, rather than impose this false consensus, brings centre stage the multiple perspectives, and possibly conflicting criteria, for success held by different parties.

In practical terms, a commitment to pluralistic evaluation involves *identifying the major parties involved in the initiative* and *comparing each with the other in terms of their perspectives.*

Different notions of success (and processes) are identified, and the strategies that different parties adopt in striving for success are identified. Success can be examined in terms of the different criteria identified.

Even here, practical issues can emerge: resources can limit the number of parties involved, and the most common combination in social work is gaining the perspectives of the social worker and their clients.

Qualitative evaluation has been associated (though this is not always the case) with an interpretivist approach, which is interested in perspectives of participants and which emphasizes a subjectivist approach as outlined in earlier chapters.

The practice process

The process of intervention, as we have seen, is the activities that are undertaken by practitioners in the conduct of intervention with, or on behalf of, the service users. At times it is defined in terms of seeking to attain certain goals, though we have seen how different notions of success – or goals – can emerge.

From an interpretivist qualitative researcher's point of view, the processes of intervention do not simply consist of activities and interactions corresponding to some objective reality. Clients' and practitioners', and other key groups', understanding of process and outcome can vary. For example, social workers, relative to clients, have a tendency to overestimate the helpfulness of insight work, the use of authority and giving advice. However, they tend to underestimate the helpfulness experienced by clients of material and financial help, and negotiations with other agencies on their behalf – that is, practical work (Sainsbury, Nixon and Phillips 1982).

Here we have pluralistic evaluation of processes as well as outcomes. An attempt should be made to document the experiences and attitudes of both clients and practitioners when describing and documenting the practice process. Reliance, for example, on the practitioner alone would potentially misrepresent the significance and impact of interventions on the client.

From the practitioner's point of view, we may often ask the questions: What were you doing and what were your reasons for doing these things? We get at the nature and rationale for their complex, often changing work. From the client's point of view, we are often concerned with: How did you experience this intervention? How did you attempt to influence what happened and with what effect? These are very general questions and issues relevant to practice evaluation of process.

Inductivism, meaning and evaluation

Qualitative evaluation methods, when they are fully interpretive, are inductive. This means that the evaluator attempts to make sense of the situation without imposing pre-existing expectations on participants. We have seen already that this means that we seek to gain an understanding by grounding our analysis in the data, and this involves using open-ended, semi-structured or unstructured interviews.

Where we evaluate in terms of certain goals, matters are not fully inductive. To do this we have to impose our own interpretations or meanings on the participants themselves. So although we may seek to identify themes about which they are concerned in relation to those goals, that is precisely what it is – in relation to those goals, which are pre-set and predetermined.

We have seen that this involves creating the understanding or meaning of participants. To do this we need to use some degree of empathic understanding. We need to be able to relate to their subjective experience – to be aware of their possible feelings, perceptions and thoughts, in the circumstances they find themselves. We need to create some sense of empathic understanding. We seek to try to picture the empirical world as it exists to those under investigation, rather than the way the researcher imagines it to be.

Some will ask how we can really fully understand and recreate the perceptions of others. We can never, in truth, fully understand the experience of another person. England (1986) argues that we have an intuitive capability of understanding others because we possess common attributes: feelings, intentions, motivations, reasoning, and so on. Thus when we listen to someone talking about their emotional state, we know what this means not because we are experiencing their emotional state, but because *we know what it feels like to experience that emotional state*. It is part of human nature, so we understand clients' (for example) accounts, because we are able to place them in context, with the information they give us, and because we know what it is like to be angry, to feel despair, to be hopeful, and the like.

What does this mean for our methodological approach? Well just like seeking to understand, describe and explain, which we discussed in Chapter Nine, we need to be using methods typical of the qualitative researcher, but with the notion of evaluation in mind. We have already seen that this can be:

- fully interpretive – when we are fully inductive and ground our analysis entirely on the themes emerging from the data
- partially interpretive – when we evaluate, using qualitative methodology, in relation to some general goals of the intervention or programme.

The more you seek to create their understanding of their world, the more the issue of depth arises. Qualitative studies generally aim at restricted samples with relatively few questions. They seek depth. There are no rules to tell evaluators how much depth and detail they require, although we would certainly, in interviews say, be looking at unstructured or semi-structured interviews (observation and documentation obviously also provide routes for qualitative research).

But how deep is deep? Open-ended interviewing can take a great deal of time and produce volumes of narrative data. They can focus on general questions, such as 'What are the characteristic ways you try to cope with Jimmy's behaviour? Or with caring for your sister's terminal cancer?' or 'How far do you think your nurse/health visitor/social worker, etc. responds to your needs?'

My research teams have conducted interviews where the time taken can be as much as two and a half to three hours (leaving those involved, we may conjecture, fuzzy-headed, cross-eyed and sweating). They can take as little as half an hour. The point is that where you seek to gain detail, you get a great deal more opportunity for understanding. The more detail we have the more we can understand and contextualize what is said (provided information is based on the intelligent process of interview, observation or documentary analysis).

Within interviews, the use of open-ended questions is important and characterizes qualitative evaluation research. This enables us to go through the process of the search for meaning from the interviewee's point of view. It enables us to minimize the imposition of predetermined responses when gathering data. This means that the question should allow the person being interviewed to respond in their own terms. This is not as straightforward as it may appear.

Take the example: *'How satisfied are you with this intervention?'* This is an outcome question. On the surface this seems an open-ended question, allowing the subject to respond along broad lines. It does not impose a range of possible alternatives (e.g. very satisfied to very dissatisfied) from which the individual must choose. However, even in a qualitative sense, even using their own words and perspectives, it is clear that the dimension along which the respondent can answer is already identified – they are asked about the degree of satisfaction. The concept of satisfaction is the concept to which they must adhere.

Of course, they might respond in relation to the issue of satisfaction. But what if the concept of satisfaction is not the one they would employ to describe their feelings or perspectives of intervention? Their response has been narrowly limited by the framing of the question. The truly open-ended question does not presuppose which dimension of feeling, analysis or thought will be salient for the interview. A better question might be *'What did you think of the nurse's/health visitor's/social worker's intervention?'* This allows the respondent to respond along whichever dimensions they choose. It could be about the personality of the practitioner. It could be about their degree of commitment (did they go out of their way to see the client when needed?). It could be about their competence, or perceptions of their knowledge of the area. Or it could be any one of a number of areas. The only confining element of the question is the request to give some kind of opinion, and that this should be about nurse/health visitor/social work intervention as they experienced it.

Like the question on satisfaction, when we focus on goals, even using qualitative methods, we are determining the dimension/domain in which the subject is expected to frame their response. This is the partially interpretive approach I have outlined earlier. Within the domain of concern (which is already set) they are able to develop their own themes and perspectives, but it is within those domains.

In either case, but particularly with the fully interpretive approach, the identification of themes, and hence the process of evaluation, occurs through a research process of content analysis. Content analysis is very much part of the process of evaluation, and hence evaluative research in this tradition.

Observation and evaluation

The primary strength of observational data is that it is collected in the field, where the action is, so to speak, and is directly observed by the evaluator. What does it add specifically to evaluation?

- By directly observing a programme, the evaluator is better able to understand the context within which intervention occurs.

- Observation lends itself to an inductive approach, learning from the grounding gained by actually being there, rather than any prior conceptualization – it can therefore aid the interpretivist qualitative evaluation approach, where we do not seek to impose interpretations or meanings on others (although we may ask whether, where it is you that is doing the observing, you would be putting your interpretation on matters right from the start).

- You can learn about things that participants in a programme may be unwilling to talk about in interview or has escaped their conscious awareness. Interviews rely, in that respect, on second-hand information.

- Evaluators can move beyond the selective perceptions of others, given in interview, although even observers are reporting their own perceptions.

Observation, in other words, gives you a kind of 'direct line' to the processes, and sometimes the outcomes, of intervention.

Of course, not all evaluation lends itself well to observation – for example where individual therapy sessions are being undertaken, particularly on sensitive areas such as sexual abuse. In these circumstances ethical considerations, as well as the overwhelming primacy of the therapy, and the potential for disruption by an external researcher, makes observation an unattractive option.

Processes and outcomes

Qualitative approaches emphasizing the importance of the subject, perceptions and meaning tend to eschew any involvement in quantitative data. However, there are those who seek to combine quantitative and qualitative methodologies, either:

- using one (qualitative) for examining processes, and the other (quantitative) for measuring outcomes, or

- mixing the two in relation to both processes and outcomes.

These researchers could be considered partly interpretivist (in my earlier terminology) or even partly objectivist.

We might seek to measure outcomes quantitatively in terms of factors like: whether a child has had to enter into care, whether they have had to be placed on the child protection register (or, indeed, whether they have been taken off the child protection register), whether they have (re-)offended, and so on. What we are here doing is matching some process of intervention to some kind of outcome. The process may involve identifying key facets of the intervention process, and the outcomes could be measured as above (these are service-based outcomes – i.e. measured in terms of service measures).

We can also mix quantitative and qualitative measures of processes. This was what I did in the partnership study elements of the depressed mothers research (Sheppard 2001, 2002). Here I used, on the one hand, a fully structured instrument looking at key facets of partnership, and related this to the presence of depression. This showed that depressed women were more likely to have partnership difficulties with the social worker. However, there was also detailed semi-structured interviews with the women on the quality of intervention, in which the problem of communication, and skills dealing with depression, came to the fore. Women were likely to be taciturn, reluctant to say what they really felt, and to agree with the social worker, going away dissatisfied while the social worker thought things were fine. Alternatively, the sense of self-blame left the women with a burning feeling of anger, which made them aggressive and partnership difficult. More is given on multiple methods in the next chapter.

Another point worth noting is that the practice process is generally complex with a variety of strands to it. It is very often difficult to disentangle one strand from another, particularly in terms of the effects each had on the outcome of the intervention. Suppose we find that young mothers involved in parenting skills programmes did have a reduction in their child care problems, and an improvement in their parenting skills. This may be down to the parenting programme. However, at the same time, all may have been the subject of direct health visitor or social work intervention, providing counselling and advice. There may be other aspects to the process: for example, they may be part of a parents' group, or may have been given enabling help to deal better with material and practical problems. Which of these strands led to the good outcome? Was it the parenting skills programme? Or was it some other aspect of the intervention? Indeed, was it in fact the growth in confidence that emerged as a result of the combination of all these facets? These are difficult to disentangle, and there are those who consider health or (in particular) social work to be too complex to disentangle one strand from another. If, therefore, we are looking to identify the 'key factor' that led to some positive outcome, in practice this may be impossible. What we are engaging in, in social work, some would argue, is making well-informed inferences, or speculating, based on detailed understanding of the processes of intervention and circumstances of clients. We can never aspire to a real 'cause and effect' analysis of effectiveness (the cause being some social work process, and the effect being the outcome). We can only use evaluative research to become well informed.

An example of this sort of thing – the multiple dimension of social work research, if not entirely qualitative analysis of processes – comes from probation research. A project evaluated by Roberts (1989) contained elements of offence-related group work, problem solving, development of social skills through drama and role play, and an introduction to purposeful activities. Offenders also had weekly contact with the probation officer and they were encouraged to get involved in voluntary work. Frankly, in such circumstances, and where a good outcome occurs, you might as well ask the client (and practitioner) their opinion as to which were the most influential aspects of the programme.

Question: Are techniques of qualitative evaluation in research of any use to practitioners in their conduct of practice?

Conclusion

We can now see an entirely different tradition in evaluation research from that characterized by the experimental design. Quite different processes are involved, and quite different dimensions of practice, as well as measurement, are valued by the qualitative researcher. Much of the qualitative research (though by no means all) is characterized by an interpretivist approach, and we need to be aware, as we have shown in this chapter, of the kinds of assumptions made by interpretivists in the conduct of their research. These assumptions are, after all, being incorporated into the knowledge applied to practice, where information based on this approach is used.

We have, however, also alluded to approaches that seek to join different methods together (rather than seeing them oppositionally), and it is to these that we shall turn next.

Exercises

10.1 Some issues that can be discussed after reading this chapter

- What is evaluation? What are the two forms of evaluation?

- What is the use of interpretivist evaluation?

- How do service user/client perspective studies fit into the qualitative tradition?

- What is the significance of pluralist qualitative evaluation?

- What place does observation have in qualitative evaluation?

10.2 An exercise using an article employing qualitative evaluation
Consider one of the following:

Hill, A. (2001) 'No one else could understand: Women's experience of a support group run by mothers of sexually abused children.' *British Journal of Social Work 21*, 3, 385–398.

Clark, A., Barbour, R. and McIntyre, P. (2002) 'Preparing for change in the secondary prevention of coronary heart disease: A qualitative evaluation of cardiac rehabilitation within a region of Scotland.' *Journal of Advanced Nursing 39*, 6, 589–598.

- Outline the background to the study and problem formulation.

- Examine the methods used. What are their strengths, limitations and appropriateness for the issues addressed? Why qualitative rather than some other evaluative form?

- What are the findings? Are there gaps?

- What are the conclusions to the study? Are they justified by the evidence?

- Do the authors identify the limits to the study?

- How useful is the study for practice? Are there any features of the methodology we should bear in mind when using these findings in practice?

Examples of research employing qualitative evaluation

Brannstrom, B., Tibbin, A. and Lowenberg, C. (2000) 'Counselling group for spouses of elderly demented patients: A qualitative evaluation study.' *International Journal of Nursing Practice 6*, 183–191.

Clark, A., Barbour, R. and McIntyre, P. (2002) 'Preparing for change in the secondary prevention of coronory heart disease: A qualitative evaluation of cardiac rehabilitation within a region of Scotland.' *Journal of Advanced Nursing 39*, 6, 589–598.

Field, D., Ingleton, L. and Clark, D. (1997) 'The cost of unpaid labour: The use of voluntary staff in the Kings Mill Hospice.' *Health and Social Care in the Community 5*, 3, 198–208.

Gould, N. (1999) 'Developing an approach to qualitative audit in inter disciplinary child protection practice.' *Child Abuse Review 8*, 193–199.

Hill, A. (2001) 'No one else could understand: Women's experiences of a support group run by and for mothers of sexually abused children.' *British Journal of Social Work 31*, 385–397.

Further reading

Cheetham, J., Fuller, R., McIvor, G. and Petch, A. (1992) *Evaluating Social Work Research*. Buckingham: Open University Press.

Gould, N. (1999) 'Qualitative Practice Evaluation.' In I. Shaw and J. Lishman (eds) *Evaluation and Social Work Practice*. London: Sage.

Kushner, S. (2000) *Personalising Evaluation*. London: Sage.

Patton, M. (1987) *How to Use Qualitative Method in Evaluation*. Newbury Park, CA: Sage.

Patton, M. (1990) *Qualitative Evaluation and Research Methods*. Newbury Park, CA: Sage.

Shaw, I. (1999) *Qualitative Evaluation*. London: Sage.

Shaw, I. and Lishman, J. (1999) *Evaluation in Social Work Practice*. London: Sage.

CHAPTER ELEVEN
Multimethod Research

One of the favoured approaches to conducting research in health and social work is the use of multiple methods. The idea is that each provides something different, but complementary. The result is (in theory) that we have more robust research with more robust findings than we would have using one method alone.

Multimethod research cuts across qualitative and quantitative research methods, and indeed different methods within those traditions. So we can end up using in-depth interviews alongside observational techniques, as well as survey techniques alongside qualitative interviews. The former of these – using different qualitative techniques together – is not generally disapproved of, even amongst purist qualitative researchers. Ethnographers are happy to use in-depth interviews alongside observation techniques (for example). But there are those who are unhappy to cut across both quantitative and qualitative techniques because, it is claimed, they operate on such different views of both research and the world that they contradict each other:

- **Quantitative research** is associated with an objective view of the world, with an emphasis on behaviour and events as being caused and on the use of deductive logic for discovery.

- **Qualitative research** is associated with a subjective view of the world, with an emphasis on human behaviour as being voluntary rather than caused and on the use of inductive logic for discovery.

Others, however, dismiss these differences, for practical purposes, suggesting the most significant facets are the complementary nature of the two approaches (Bryman 1988).

Objectivists see the world as external to the individual. It exists independent of the individuals, or subjects, who view it. It is 'out there', has a real existence, and in principle, using appropriate techniques, we are able to discover it. *Subjectivists*, on the other hand, consider there is no objective reality out there waiting to be discovered. The world is only to be understood from the perspective of those involved in whatever phenomenon that is being studied. And these people may have widely diverging views about what is going on. Who is to decide which of these views is the accurate one? (Of course there is no one accurate view, but just a number of perspectives.)

Causation sees people's behaviour as the product of certain forces or influences on the world, some of which they do not recognize. Of course, in social science things are not that simple and, since there can be multiple causation, not all of which we may be aware of, the notion of probability comes to play – probabilistic causation. *Voluntarists* consider that we undertake actions of our own accord, and that, therefore, we decide and determine what we do. We do something because we choose to do so.

Deductive theorizing is the process of theory testing. You make a hypothesis of some kind of relationship (e.g. people who are abused as children are more likely to be abusers as adults), and you then set about testing this relationship by seeking to relate two variables: the experience of being abused in the past, and the act of abuse now. *Inductive* theorizing involves not starting with any assumptions about relationships. Instead the researcher begins with a broad question – say parenting – and then seeks to interview or observe individuals, gradually teasing out the key issues on the basis of what they discover.

Now, all these approaches have merit. However, the argument is not so much about their merit (although some qualitative researchers will dismiss the value of quantitative research and vice versa), it is more about whether the positions are mutually exclusive. Those who think they are consider that the views of the world are so different from each other that they cannot be combined. Those who consider they can be used together tend to think that polarization is not helpful. They believe, for example, that:

- human actions can be both voluntary *and* caused

- to understand the world we need to incorporate individuals' perspectives, but we *can* get to some objective view by finding the most plausible, internally coherent and all-embracing explanation

- both deductive *and* inductive methods can be used together, and that, in fact, humans tend to use both methods together.

From the point of view of health and social work research, we are often concerned with the evaluation, in whatever way, of practice. There has been a wide tendency to use multiple methods for this purpose, on the basis that particular methods are capable of telling only part of the story. If we want to get the most comprehensive view possible, then it makes sense to use the widest range of methods, which will enable us to get at different aspects of a situation.

In essence, this basically pragmatic approach to research involves seeking to get the best out of particular methods. What is it that each of these methods have to offer us? One important way of looking at multimethod research and the ways different methods might be used together is to examine some of the things each tradition can actually do:

- What can quantitative research do that qualitative cannot?

- What can qualitative research do that quantitative does not?

- If each does different things, is there room to consider that they may be complementary to each other, rather than have a negative view that they do entirely different things and approach a different reality?

What can quantitative research do and how?

Magnitude

Magnitude is one of the things with which quantitative methods can provide us. Quantitative methods itemize a number of variables, each of which may be applied to a population group. Classically, this involves us in the use of fully structured instruments, which we discussed earlier in the sequence. Magnitude can provide two types of measures:

- the number of subjects/people/participants who fall into a particular category

- the strength or the degree in which they fall into that category.

Thus, for example, we can find out, by asking participants, whether or not they feel they have been unwell in the last four weeks. This question seeks to get at personal and lay perceptions of well-being. They may be given yes and no as alternatives, or a box to tick if they have felt unwell. From that individual response (and this will in all likelihood only be one of a number of variables looked at in the instrument) we can then go on to a particular population by aggregating (adding together) the individual responses. So, if we are looking at the population of Plymouth, we might survey all adults and find (as an arbitrary statement) that 44 per cent answered yes to that question and 56 per cent answered no. From this we begin to get an idea of the scale of the problem in Plymouth.

However, this involves a simple binary response. If we look at this in terms of scale, we can identify the strength of that response. It may remain the case that 44 per cent felt, to some degree, unwell in the previous four weeks. However, we do not know the extent to which they felt unwell. Some may have felt mildly unwell, while others had, what they felt, were life-threatening diseases. We might therefore ask them to respond in the following terms:

mildly unwell

mildly to moderately unwell

moderately unwell

moderately to seriously unwell

seriously unwell

These could be assessed on a scale, and we might find that the majority of those who said they were unwell felt mildly, or mildly to moderately, unwell. This might change matters considerably. We might find that three out of four of those who said they felt unwell considered they were less than moderately unwell. This would only leave 11 per cent of the total population surveyed saying that they felt moderately unwell or worse.

The point about the second approach is that it gives two kinds of magnitude:

- the magnitude in *numbers* who felt unwell
- the magnitude in the *extent* to which they felt unwell, or the severity of these feelings.

In focusing on magnitude, quantitative research is able to provide a precise number over a total population. Why is this important?

Well it's important from a research point of view because we can state more precisely the nature and degree of the problem. We might qualitatively state that there are few, some or many people who were interviewed who said they were unwell; but such a qualitative statement is extremely vague. Yet this is the way in which many qualitative researchers write. Quantitative data, on the other hand, allows a precise statement of scale.

It is also important from a practical point of view. This is an issue of particular concern to those in a profession like social work, or the health professionals. Take this issue of subjective feelings of health and ill health. What would you do, when planning services, if you were told that there were some, a few or many people who felt unwell over a given four-week period? How are you supposed to respond to that? 'Oh well, I'll develop some, a few or many services in response'! Subjective feelings of ill health could well affect a range of important issues: the capacity of parents to care for their children, the use of health provision, the willingness of people to go to work, and when there, their capacity to carry out their work. If I were a health or social care manager I would want a more precise statement of the scale of the problem before I committed resources to it. This is precisely what quantitative data allows. We can say that 11 per cent felt moderately to seriously unwell and seek to develop appropriate services on that basis.

Of course, that is not in itself enough for the development of services. We might want to know the nature of their ill health, whether they used existing services, what those services did, and what they did if they did not use existing services. We might also ask them, where they did not use services, what would help improve uptake. And so on.

Association and correlation

Quantitative measures do not end there. We do not simply have the option of presenting simple findings. We can look at matters in more detail. Let's take some of the practical concerns of our public health specialists in Plymouth. They may be interested in the overall results – the 11 per cent who were moderately or more ill. However, they are also likely to be interested in which groups reported which level of ill health.

We could look at it in various ways. Are, for example, women likely to feel more or less ill health than men? If, say, women said they felt moderate or more severe ill health at a rate of 15 per cent and men reported this only at a level of 7 per cent, this might have implications for the targeting of resources. The same could be said about class. We know ill health is more frequent in poorer, more deprived groups than those who are better off. So we might find such groups reporting higher levels of subjective feelings of moderate ill health or worse. We could also expect that particular local areas would have different levels of subjective feelings of ill health, with the least affluent areas being the worst affected. Examining these different trends would have the practical advantages of allowing us to target more effectively. Rather than some generalized notion of 11 per cent throughout the city, we would have 'hot spots' where the targeting would most effectively take place.

However, these kinds of data provide further opportunities both in practice and academic terms. We can see here the possibility of relationships between, respectively, sex and ill health, class and ill health, and environment and ill health (subjectively assessed). *Quantitative data, in other words, enables us to begin to identify relationships between different elements.* These are generally referred to as empirical generalizations: relationships that we would expect to see regularly, not just in Plymouth, but in Manchester, London, and even perhaps Chicago.

However, we can go further than mere correlations. We can begin to look at causation. We might be interested in the question: What is it that leads to people feeling higher levels of ill health? Of course we could hypothesize that actual ill health leads to feelings of ill health. But we might also hypothesize that sex-related socialization processes have an impact on subjective feelings of health or illness. Thus we could suggest that men are socialized into not admitting 'weakness', and this leads them to deny feelings of ill health. This would require us to look at their attitudes – about men and women and health – but it also involves the 'when' question. The general idea is that for one thing to cause another, or at least to have a causal relationship (there might be other causes as well), it should precede it (i.e. for A to cause B, A needs to precede B). If, for example, we were trying to establish a relationship between the experience of abuse as a child, and depression as an adult, this has the particular advantage that the experience of abuse clearly precedes the depression as an adult.

Measures of association and correlation have the advantage, furthermore, of allowing us to establish the magnitude of the relationship. Not everyone who becomes depressed may have experienced abuse as a child, and not everyone experiencing abuse as a child will become depressed. Furthermore, we can see the extent to which experience of abuse, as opposed to other factors (for example, educational achievement), had a causal effect on depression. It may be, for example, that while depression is associated with the experience of abuse as a child, where high levels of academic performance occurs this association disappears.

Generalizability

One important feature of research is the issue of the extent to which we can generalize from a study to a total population. How far, for example, can we extrapolate from one study of Plymouth to suggest that it reflects Plymouth as a whole? How far can we tell that a study, say, of Exeter and a London borough accurately informs us about the state of things in the country as a whole?

REPRESENTATIVENESS

The key here is the issue of representativeness – the extent to which the study population can be considered to be like the wider populations about which we wish to comment. If we are trying to suggest that social services departments react to referrals for possible child abuse in certain kinds of ways, how can we know the information from our study, which indicates they do react in a particular way, is representative of things over the country as a whole? This is no idle question. One study by Gibbons and her colleagues (1995) indicated that for every seven such referrals that went through child protection procedures, only one went on to the child protection register. Given the emotional pain attached to this process, such findings are very important. It might suggest that social services departments were taking an altogether too conservative approach to referrals, and that a 'lighter touch' would be better. Perhaps the damage done to families outweighed the advantages of such a wide-ranging trawl of referrals.

Some qualitative researchers would suggest that the search for representativeness, or the capacity to generalize from a study, is not their business. Their case study approach allows them to comment only on the case being studied. However, for health or social work, which seeks some sort of practical application, this is not helpful.

One way we can seek to justify this is in terms of the character of the study or the study population. We could, for example, suggest that, in a study of a single social services department, the way in which it operates is so similar to other social services departments that the findings are generally applicable. This is not such a bad position. Much of social services work is governed by the same general rules. The law, for example, requires that social services identify those at risk of serious harm, and those in need. Social services also are generally characterized by specialist child care services, separate from adult services. They are expected, furthermore, to have an assessment process at the point of referral. We can also see if, socio-demographically, the population studied and other populations are similarly deprived. Even some of these require quantitative data: most obviously on socio-demographic data.

There is nothing wrong with this approach, and many have adopted it. However, there are ways in which we can seek representativeness through sampling. We can sample particular types of local authority. The government has now identified types of local authority, and it would be possible to select a group of local authorities that is representative of all in chosen characteristics. These characteristics are based on quantitative measures of local population, type of service provision, and so on.

In social science we also have our general sampling techniques. We can identify, as we have seen, stratified or random samples that will enable us systematically to establish the degree to which our study population is representative of the wider population. This can be done through these sampling processes, but we can also check against the characteristics of the wider population; for example: Are there the same proportions of men and women? Do the age ranges correspond? And so on. We can also identify the degree of confidence we can have that the findings really are representative. We get this with election polls, which suggest that we can have confidence in the findings plus or minus 5 per cent.

Likewise, we can have confidence that other areas of study are representative in the same way.

REPLICABILITY

Replicability refers to the capacity for a study to be repeated, under exactly the same conditions (e.g. Vaughn and Leff 1976). Where we have quantitative methods of this sort, we are able to reproduce the same kind of study a second time. We could, for example, produce a second random sample, or identify a different, but still representative, group of social services, and carry out a similar study. Because our findings have the advantage of precision, we can, in principle, check that the first findings really are accurate for the wider population. Would a second study of child protection processes again show that only one in seven cases led to registration on the child protection register? This again is important because it indicates the degree of reliability with which we can hold the findings – a study in principle repeatable is in principle falsifiable; that is, we can prove it wrong. In reality, studies in social science are almost never replicable, but it is the *principle* of replicability which is held to be important.

Outcome and change – quantitative

Outcome and change are particularly important aspects of the evaluative repertoire of all human services. Where we want to evaluate particular programmes or approaches to intervention, it helps to know what happens. The capacity of quantitative research to focus on magnitude is again an advantage in this respect. If we want to look at change, it helps to know what has changed and how much it has changed. Magnitude involves numbers, and numbers (of course) are quantitative.

So what does this involve? Let's first think of practice generally. You want to know if your clients have improved over, say, a six-month period. You may wish to look at their interaction with their children as a key aspect of their parenting. One way of looking at that is to see whether the number of times the mother plays with the child each day has increased in six months. If it has, this might give some grounds for optimism that matters are improving (although it may only be one measure – you hope the increase in time together does not lead to an increase in arguments or corporal punishment).

It's the same with research. Let's take depression. Suppose we wanted to see whether a particular intervention – say a support group at a family centre, or intensive visiting by a community psychiatric nurse – had an effect on the level of depression suffered by single mothers. We might have a baseline–follow-up set of measures. That is, a measure at the start of the intervention, and a measure at six months. We might find that, while 100 per cent of women were depressed at the start (it's a depressed women's group), this was only the case with 75 per cent of women at follow-up. We might take matters further – what about a year, or 18 months? Is the improvement sustained? We might find that after 12 and 18 months a steady group of 20 per cent remained not depressed, suggesting that for some, but not all, the improvement was maintained.

Such data again provide us with a clear idea of effect. However, of course, we don't know that this is a natural effect, one that would have occurred anyway. A quarter of these women might have improved regardless at 6, 12 and 18 months. That is why we need a comparison group of those who did not receive that intervention. As we saw with experimental designs, the issues surrounding this are complex, but the basic idea of the comparison is to provide good grounds to believe that what we thought caused the change (the support group) actually was the cause of the change, and not some random or normal process of development.

The point is that quantitative work provides some precision to the nature and degree of change (or maintenance) that occurs. We can say that social work intervention holds some families stable, or improves the situation, and the degree to which both achieve this. This is a central issue for activities such as social work – otherwise, why bother?

What can qualitative research do and how?

Gaining meanings

One of the key elements associated with qualitative methods is its capacity to see things through the eyes of the participants in the study. If we look at mothers caring for their children we can find out what they see are the main issues. If we ask the children, we can see what they see as the main issue. And, of course, they won't necessarily see things in the same ways. Where, for example, we are looking at relationships between teenagers and their mothers, it would not be unusual for teenagers to consider their mothers to be over-restrictive (particularly teenage girls) and for the mothers to consider the teenagers difficult, moody and rebellious.

What qualitative methods allow us to do is explore these perspectives in a grounded way. Grounded, in these circumstances, means grounding our approach on the data collected, and seeking to make as few assumptions as possible when setting up the project. This kind of approach is associated with unstructured interviews and direct observation, in which the researcher's effort is to try to avoid influencing the information gained from participants. So with direct observational methods the researcher seeks to blend in as much as possible in the background, even doing research incognito. With interviews, the idea of the interviewee 'rambling' (i.e. going in whatever direction they like, saying what they want) is also encouraged. The idea is that, in this process, the researcher allows, as far as possible, the participant to set the agenda. This is the exact antithesis of what is done by the quantitative researcher with their pre-set questionnaires, with clear set alternatives available in answers.

Access to meanings (i.e. the ways others see the world) may be less difficult to gain than some qualitative researchers suggest. If the meanings adopted by the researcher and participants were so different it would imply that the participant meanings would be pretty inaccessible to the researcher, and it would be difficult for the researcher not to influence things with their own agenda. If they were not so different then, of course, there is not so much of a problem.

What we are talking of here is an inductive approach. However, two points are worth mentioning:

1.　Just like in quantitative approaches (and despite the claims of its most extreme adherents to the contrary), we cannot but have an impact on participants. In unstructured qualitative research, the researcher has to prompt, and even mild comments of approval or disapproval can affect the research process. Likewise, the quantitative researcher tries to screen out their influence by using pre-set questions and interview processes. Their influence, as we have seen, is already manifest through having created the questionnaires in the first place.

2.　Most researchers combining quantitative and qualitative research do use semi-structured qualitative interviews. This means that, in general terms, issues are decided in advance, but the content of the participants' responses to those issues is, as much as possible, determined by them. We may, for example, want to look at the problems women have with child care. This issue, or area, is set. However, the ways in which the responses are made and framed can be decided by the women themselves in the course of the interview.

Where multimethod, quantitative/qualitative research is being used, therefore, there is less of a move towards extremes, but an attempt to meet in the middle.

Depth and flexibility

Qualitative researchers make much of the depth and flexibility of their approach. They often speak of 'rich' data, of its being layered or textured (whatever that means), so that it sounds a bit like a lasagne! They do, though, have a point. With the deductive approach of quantitative research, everything is set in advance, and there is almost no room for flexibility. You can only look at the pre-set variables and measure them in the ways allowed in the instruments. The possible relationships between variables are also pre-set. You might decide to look at the relationship between maternal depression and child care problems. That will be the only thing you can look at because that is all your instruments allow.

With qualitative methods you can move between areas more flexibly. You may be interested in depression and child care problems, but you can explore them in terms of issues that might additionally emerge. How, for example, do women understand their depression? Is this something they regard as a fact of life, something they just have to put up with? Or is it painful, something they wish to get rid of as quickly as possible? Because you are asking them about these matters, they are able to answer in their own way, and you can follow them in the direction they choose to go. They are not limited by tick boxes, but by the extent to which they wish to explore the matters at hand.

The same goes for depth. Where you have a general area in which you are interested, there is nothing to stop you, and the participants, from exploring that area in as much depth as you like (in so far as other demands allow). There is nothing about the interview itself that prevents this from happening. We can take an example from my research (Sheppard 2001). Here we initially wished to look at the accuracy with which social workers identified depression in their clients. They did not seem to do that well, but we soon found out that this was the wrong question. Rather the issue was how they defined the personality of the mother. It became clear that their central concern with risk (to the child) meant that all matters were overlaid by their concern about risk. Thus they incorporated depression into a framework for thinking about mothers that included risk. Hence it emerged that there were three categories:

1.   *Troubled and troublesome*: Women who were essentially self-regarding, concerned with their own needs, for whom

depression was allied to a high level of egocentricity. These characteristics helped make the risk to the child higher than might otherwise be the case.

2. *Genuinely depressed:* Women who found it difficult to cope with their children. This was connected with their depression, which both disabled them with child care, and made the performance of child care more difficult. They recognized their child's needs and did not put their needs ahead of the child. This meant that the risk to the child was less (although still problematic).

3. *Stoics:* Women who, though depressed, seemed to be able to 'manage in adversity'. Their depression held them back, but they still coped (with the consequence that they were least likely to get resources).

Importantly, these divisions had implications for intervention, in that the troubled and troublesome group were likely to be more closely monitored and get more resources, while the stoics got the least resources, and little monitoring.

Here is a case where qualitative interviewing enabled us to find out in more depth about the actions and understanding of social workers. It did not mean, however, that measurement of depression was irrelevant: we needed to identify the depressed women in order that we could ask social workers questions about them.

Outcome and change – qualitative

We have already focused on outcome measures in relation to quantitative measures. What can qualitative approaches do for us here?

Well, a point frequently made by qualitative researchers about quantitative researchers is that they presume in advance what is important, rather than the participants themselves. This is a value judgement in two ways. First, it means that it is the researcher's values that are being used to decide what should be evaluated. Second, it gives the power to decide what is important to the researcher. How can qualitative research help us with this?

Qualitative research, instead of deciding in advance what is important, has the capacity to allow the important issues to emerge from the research. This means that they are seeking to find out from participants what they consider is important and allow them to make judgements about this. Let's take my research on coping in child and family care (Sheppard 2004). We sought here to look at the coping strategies adopted by women when they were in adversity, but as a part of this, to tell us how they coped. Well, traditional ways of measuring this might be a battery of outcome measures. Did the child's behaviour improve? Did the woman's mental state improve? Did her parenting improve? And so on.

The interesting point is that that was only part of the story for these women. Some women did indeed appraise their coping in terms of outcomes – that they were able to cope better themselves, that the problems they had had diminished, and so on. Others, however, did not evaluate their coping in this way. Some women evaluated coping in terms of its continuity – that it was a long-term process, unlikely to change, and that they just carry on. Others judged their coping in terms of 'character': whether or not things improved, they showed a lot of character in dealing with it. Others judged coping in terms of their own personal growth: what they had learned for themselves as a result of their experiences. Yet others judged things in terms of their capacity to use support (and hence act wisely). Because we did not seek to decide in advance what we should measure, we had a range of different ways of evaluating outcome, derived from the women themselves, through the more flexible means of qualitative interviewing.

Of course, these are not exclusive categories. There is nothing to stop us looking at coping in both these qualitative terms and other quantitative terms. In the coping study, we carried out a six-month follow-up study of the women, focusing on changes in the levels of child care problems, of wider social problems, and levels of depression. In relation to these factors we could look at how matters had changed over the six-month period. The point is, both approaches are illuminating. There is no reason for us not to carry them out together to get a composite picture of these women's situations. The fact that they do not spontaneously talk of coping in the same ways that they were defined by researchers does not mean they were not interested in those issues. Likewise, researchers can find illuminating the kinds of ways in which women judge their coping, and this can have practical effects. For those, for example, who define the successful use of support as significant for evaluating coping, we could look to develop ways of helping women to use their supports more effectively, or to provide appropriate support groups.

Another feature of qualitative research is the capacity to focus on processes. Many researchers have a preference for using qualitative methods to focus on processes of intervention, which lead to particular outcomes. For example, in the depression study (Sheppard 2001, 2002) we spent considerable effort looking at the processes characterizing social worker/client relationships. Our general focus might be considered that of 'partnership'. In this we looked at the ways social workers defined the cases, what strategies they used, how women experienced these strategies, and how they responded to them. These are all factors that might be said to affect outcomes. Much of this was qualitative. We also, however, looked at factors that impacted on the quality of partnership, finding, for example, that high levels of psychodynamic skills were a mediating factor between depression and partnership (i.e. where women were depressed, social workers with high levels of psychodynamic skills were more likely to have better partnerships). Here is an example of where qualitative and quantitative research came together for purposes of evaluation.

Combining the qualities of the two

What do the combination of these methods offer? Well we can see how these can be used together profitably, just by recognizing how their strengths are complementary to each other. We can look at this in terms of a number of areas.

Generalizability and detail

We can take, for example, a situation where we want to draw general data from a wide area, but also have detail enabling us to have the depth that would help us understand things better.

Thus, in social work, we could, for example, choose a representative group of local authorities, and then randomly sample their populations around some key issues. Let us suggest that we want to know their predominant parenting styles. Do they believe in smacking, and how far can they go with the physical punishment of their children? The advantage of seeking to get a representative sample in this way is that we can extrapolate from the findings to the population as a whole, and thus have some clear indications of attitudes, actions and magnitude.

However, we can go from this to look in detail at some representative groups. It might be from appropriately chosen local authorities, or it may be a sample of the study population. Now, in general, costs would prevent us from carrying out detailed interviews with everybody. Thus we use quantitative instruments with the main population. However, carefully choosing some allows us to have some confidence that they are representative, yet enable us to go into some detail about the perceptions, attitudes and actions of the interview population. We have, therefore:

- a large survey of attitudes
- the detail and depth of qualitative interviews
- and the knowledge that we can have some confidence that these are representative.

Magnitude and meaning

By its very nature we are able to obtain some notion of magnitude by using quantitative data. This can be very helpful. Take, for example, my
study of women coping in adversity (Sheppard 2004). We wanted to
have some idea of how far and in what ways women used social support.
By using a social support instrument we were able to identify who felt
they had support available, whether they used that support, and how
many and who were available as supporters. However, we were also able
to examine the meaning of that support to the women. We did this
through qualitative interviews. We found out, for example, that some
women had little support but that some women preferred not to use support that was available. We found out also that the meaning of support
was often about 'listen and don't disagree with me' – that is, accept the
general framework in which I view things. Critical appraisal of actions
was not regarded as supportive, and led to non-use of support. We also
found that integration, in which they and their friends operated a mu-
tual support process, was one which characterized those women who
had the most, and the most effective, support. Thus, by using a combination of quantitative and qualitative methods, we were able to look at
both:

- the extent of support
- the meaning of the support.

We should also not place such a distance between quantitative and qualitative methods. Silverman (2000) has suggested that qualitative researchers would do well to do some rudimentary counting of what they
discover in their research. Rather than use the general terms 'some', 'a
few', or 'many', they would be better off saying 'this or that many' had
these characteristics. That would provide some measurement of the
magnitude and importance of particular types of responses.

Likewise, it behoves quantitative researchers to take account of
meaning when constructing instruments. If we want to construct instruments on women's attitudes to child care, it is a good idea that we inter-

view them first, in a more qualitative way, to find out the kinds of issues that are significant for them, and the kinds of ways they think about them. That way you are able to construct questionnaires capable of getting at both magnitude and meaning.

In some cases, researchers have suggested that instruments should be developed on the back of full-scale qualitative studies. That way, they argue, you can reach the point where we have 'scientific' findings based on properly constructed questionnaires. Most would certainly not go that far, but many see that meaning should be incorporated into instruments.

Triangulation

Triangulation is a method in social science where you seek to take information from two or more vantage points. We have spoken mostly about methodology. Hence we can use two or more methodologies, for example interviews and questionnaires, or questionnaires and participant observation. The idea is that where you use diverse methodologies, they can validate your findings. So, if you obtain similar findings using qualitative interviews and structured questionnaires, this would give you a good reason to consider it valid. Take, for example, the idea that depressed mothers have more trouble with child care than those not depressed. You might find that using instruments to detect depression and child and parenting problems. You might also do that by interviewing the mothers and asking them how they experience child care. Where these two agree, you could well say, convincingly, that child care problems are associated with depression (as indeed they are).

Triangulation is not confined to methods. It can also be used, for instance, in relation to different sources of information. So, we could bring together documentary evidence and quantitative data. Or we could ask different individuals who are able to comment on the situation. We might interview a woman and her sister (as do Bifulco and Moran 1999) about their experiences of parenting when they were children. Where there is a high degree of concordance between the two, we have greater confidence in the findings than where we have only sought information from one source.

The point here is that the different properties of different approaches mean that using two or more enables us to feel we have been more rigorous and careful in our research. Combining quantitative and qualitative methods, therefore, can have the effect of increasing our confidence in our findings.

Conclusion

Multimethod research approaches knowledge development in a manner that seeks to overcome the critical claims made by adherents to exclusively quantitative or exclusively qualitative methods. The argument, whether based on pragmatism or epistemology, is that there is no good reason why different methods should not be used together, to the benefit of the development of our understanding.

The result of this is that we have come full circle and have had to refer back to and consider issues we examined early in the book. In so doing, however, we have been able to highlight the different contributions that can be made by qualitative and quantitative research. Of course, this may be criticized by those who would argue that such multimethod approaches draw upon contradictory assumptions about the nature of the social world. Others see this as wholly defensive and narrow, and that combining these approaches provides us with a better opportunity to understand and evaluate the social world. This is very much an approach which has been outlined in this chapter.

We have now journeyed through the range of social science methods, and sought to show how, by understanding the methods used in the conduct of studies, we are better able to appraise and use those studies in practice. We know the strength and weaknesses of all these approaches, what should be undertaken when using particular methods (and hence the extent to which particular studies have used their methods appropriately and adequately), and we can better appraise the usefulness of any particular study for practice.

The practitioner, in other words, should now be in a better position critically to appraise any piece of research, and hence be able to use research in a more informed manner. It is to be hoped that this is exactly what is achieved once they have fully read this book.

Exercises

11.1 An exercise using research employing multimethod approaches
Consider one of the following:

Wilson, K., Sinclair, I. and Gibbs, L. (2000) 'The trouble with foster care: The impact of stressful events on foster carers.' *British Journal of Social Work 30*, 2, 193–210.

Komaromy, C., Sidell, M. and Katz, J. (2000) 'The quality of terminal care in residential and nursing homes.' *International Journal of Palliative Nursing 6*, 4, 192–200.

- Outline the background to the study and problem formulation.

- Why did the authors consider multimethod research was the best way to obtain the information they sought?

- Examine the methods used. What are its strengths, limitations and appropriateness for the issues addressed?

- What are the findings? Are there gaps?

- What are the conclusions to the study? Are they justified by the evidence? Do the authors identify limits to the study?

- How useful is the study for practice?

- Are there any particular facets of practice for which it is helpful?

Examples of research employing multimethod approaches

Iwaniec, D. and Snedda, H. (2002) 'The quality of parenting of individuals who have failed to thrive as children.' *British Journal of Social Work 32*, 3, 283–298.

Komaromy, C., Sidell, M. and Katz, J. (2000) 'The quality of terminal care in residential and nursing homes.' *International Journal of Palliative Nursing 6*, 4, 192–200.

Ross, F. and Tissier, J. (1997) 'The care management interface with general practice: A case study.' *Health and Social Care in the Community 5*, 3, 153–161.

Sheppard, M. (2001) *Social Work Practice with Depressed Mothers in Child and Family Care.* London: The Stationery Office. (Chapter 2: 'Context and Methods'.)

Tolsen, D., Smith, M. and Knight, P. (1999) 'An investigation of the components of best nursing practice in the care of acutely ill hospitalised older patients with coincidental dementia: A multi method design.' *Journal of Advanced Nursing 30*, 5, 1127–1134.

Waitzkin, H., Williams, R., Bock, J., McCloskey, J., Willging, C. and Wagner, W. (2002) 'Public health matters, safety net institutions buffer the impact of Medicaid managed care: A multi method assessment in a rural state.' *American Journal of Public Health 92*, 4, 598–610.

Wilson, K., Sinclair, I. and Gibbs, I. (2000) 'The trouble with foster care: The impact of stressful events on foster carers.' *British Journal of Social Work 30*, 2, 193–210.

Further reading

Brewer, J. and Hunter, A. (1989) *Multi Method Research: A Synthesis of Styles.* London: Sage.

Bryman, A. (1988) *Quantity and Quality in Social Research.* London: Unwin Hyman.

Clarke, A. and Dawson, R. (1999) *Evaluation Research.* London: Sage.

Pawson, R. and Tilley, N. (1987) *Realistic Evaluation.* London: Sage.

Afterword

We have been able to look at a wide range of methodologies, to critically appraise them, and to consider how they might be considered by the practitioner, who wishes to obtain 'best evidence'. We have also, at the outset, been able to identify the ways by which the practitioner is able to incorporate research findings into his or her conduct of everyday practice. We may now conclude up by summarizing some of the major issues that need to be considered in relation to social research. We have identified them as each relates to specific methodologies, but we can look at them now as 'issues in themselves'.

The glossary of key terms that follows this afterword lists (not in any order of priority) the major dimensions we might consider in social research, and the kinds of issues we should take into account. These social research dimensions can be considered together with the process of incorporation into practice.

We have now gone full circle. We started out by considering what it meant to be evidence-based. We identified the key elements of 'process knowledge' – the ways in which practitioners think and reason, and how this enables us to make use of social research and knowledge generally. We have reviewed the main dimensions of social research, culled from the range of methodologies used in health and social work.

It is clear now that many of the abilities required by practitioners when dealing with a case are very similar to those required when looking at research. Hence the range of analytic processes required in the conduct of practice, particularly those of critical appraisal, are very similar to those required when considering social research. We can, therefore, begin to understand the analysis and use of social research, and its application to practice, cognitively at least, as a seamless process. This does not mean that the process is straightforward. We are here talking about high-level cognitive abilities that would be needed to conduct good, knowledge, or evidence- or research-based practice.

This, however, is the stuff of degree learning, and emphasizes the suitability of higher education for health and social work professions (as if such emphasis were needed). What is needed of the informed practitioner is not just that they know the relevant research, but that they know how to interpret that research, in terms of what it has on offer, and its strengths and weaknesses.

This book has, I hope, given professionals in health and social work, and students in these areas, both an education through which they will be better able to use that research, and a handbook to refer to when seeking to use research. In the process, it is hoped that a contribution has been made to create a reality out of the desire for knowledge or evidence- or research-based practice.

Glossary of Key Terms in Social Research

Inductive versus deductive procedures. This is about the ways in which researchers proceed in their development of knowledge. Inductive procedures involve the researcher in steeping themselves in the data, from which themes, concepts and theories may emerge. It is essentially data first, concepts, theories and themes later. Deductive procedures occur where the researcher proposes, at the outset, a relationship between two, or more, dimensions of social life. We may relate female depression to social class, proposing that 'female depression is higher in working-class women than in middle class women'. Here the proposition comes first, and the data collection follows. The data in turn are used to confirm or falsify the proposition.

Causal explanations versus voluntarism. Human behaviour or actions can be attributed to some external 'force'. In such cases, the behaviour would be said to be, in some way, caused. Where, for example, we suggest that poor parenting is the result of a parent having experienced abuse when they themselves were a child, we would suggest that there is an external cause for the parenting: the experience of abuse as a child. The same would go for stress-related behaviour – the parent who loses their temper against their child after a series of negative events (e.g. financial problems, losses in their life) may be said to be acting in a way that has been caused by stress. Where an individual seeks to 'play down' an injury to their child, we may suggest this is voluntary, and the key notion here is that of 'reasons'. We would suggest that they had reasons for acting in this way – that they feared their child might be 'taken away' if the authorities considered the injury to be non-accidental.

Object(ive) versus subject(ive). These represent different ways of viewing the social world. In the first case – viewing it as objective – social researchers believe they are able, using the right procedures, to apprehend clearly and objectively the social world. They are dealing in 'social facts'. There are x number of suicides, so many people are depressed, and so on. On the other hand, there are those who see an essentially subjective reality, in which the world is socially or personally constructed. Child abuse is not an unproblematic, objective 'thing', it is a name for a set of activities that have been defined in a certain (and negative) way. Thus we find phrases, not so long ago widely considered to be appropriate for child care, to be indicators of child abuse today, such as 'spare the rod and spoil the child' (or, less so, 'children should be seen and not heard').

Generalizable and non-generalizable. Where research is said to be generalizable, it is considered that findings may be applied generally, and that the findings (and the study group) are representative of that particular area of interest generally (such as findings related to mental health rates, the needs of older people, or parenting beliefs). In other cases social researchers do not set out to generalize. They may seek, at an extreme, only to make claims about the particular focus of study itself. For example, an ethnographic study of one particular school, or social services office, would be considered to be just that: simply an analysis and representation of one place. Indeed, they may even argue that the nature of the social world is so complex that you cannot obtain a picture that is representative in the way the more statistically minded would claim.

Representative and non-representative. The last point represents extremes of 'positions in principle' about social research, many other researchers may be seeking representativeness, and achieve greater or lesser levels of representativeness in any particular study. Those who seek to obtain statistical representativeness will do so through appropriate sampling techniques, most ideally random or stratified random sampling. Another way of achieving representativeness would be to identify characteristics in the study 'site' that are common to similar 'sites'. For example, if you study one particular form of practice (say, in child care), you may claim certain characteristics of the office or team – such as that they are a specialist team, or that they are responding to the same legislation, and so on, as indicators of representativeness. For those of a statistical persuasion, this may not be ideal, but it provides 'reasons to believe' that the group, and findings, are representative. Further down the scale would be research undertaken where the researcher was unable to identify any clear ways in which the study undertaken was representative.

Theoretical versus statistical sampling. Those who use statistical sampling do so in order to achieve representativeness in a group (see above). It is very much associated with deductive approaches (theory testing), although it does not have to be (for example, this could form part of a data set that can be analysed for themes, from which concepts or empirical generalizations may emerge). Theoretical sampling is a form of sample through which the researcher seeks to obtain and interrogate data based on the emerging development of themes. For example, in looking at social work practice, they may find an emerging theme around the 'hand-over' between daytime and out-of-hours social work teams. In order to look closer at this, the researcher may focus on the period between 4p.m. and 5.30p.m. each day, during which interactions related to hand-overs are more likely to take place.

Standardized and unstandardized. This refers to approaches to interviews. Standardized interviews are associated with quantitative research, and present the respondent with pre-set alternatives. Much emphasis is placed on making sure that the presentation (including that by the interviewer) is exactly the same in relation to each respondent, in order that findings are uncontaminated by sources of bias. Hence there are rules of interview conduct that must be adhered to. The emphasis is on 'exactly the same for everyone'. Unstandardized interviews are qualitative, and involve the minimum identification of themes. Considerable effort is made to engage the subject or participant in the process, so the interview flows in the directions they dictate. This is also associated with the subject defining their own issues and concerns in a language, and with assumptions of their own. Proponents of unstandardized interviews also argue that they seek to achieve minimum contamination, and achieve this by not pre-setting, or presuming, the issues of concern, the ways they should be defined, or how they should be measured.

Interviews as **discrete interactions versus unproblematic forums** for data gathering. Some researchers regard the interview itself as a discrete activity, which should be part of the analysis of data as much as the data produced by the interview. The interview is an interaction involving personalities, who may have their own perceptions and issues, and bring their own interpretations of the nature and purpose of research and interviews. This 'discrete interaction' view encourages what is called reflexivity – the examination of self, and context as a means of understanding data produced. Others consider this vastly exaggerated, and that provided they are conducted properly, the exchange of information, and understanding that exchange, is far less problematic than the 'discrete interview' people would maintain.

Reliability and validity. Reliability and validity, as twin concepts, are associated with quantitative research, and relate to questionnaire development. A questionnaire is valid to the extent that it focuses on the subject that it purports to focus on. It is reliable to the extent that it will produce the same results in the same circumstances (i.e. that it can be relied upon to be consistent from one use to another). Validity is often used by qualitative researchers also, but in a different way. Here, for example, researchers may be concerned that their findings are valid. They may wish to be sure that the themes that have emerged from interviews or observation are a true reflection of the themes in the lived lives of the subjects or participants. Hence they may present findings back to the participants to discover whether they recognize and agree with the themes.

Insider and outsider. Insiders are those who conduct research who have 'particular insight' into the issues by dint of being a member of a class of subjects or participants with whom the research is being conducted. When research is conducted with nurses, where it is conducted by a nurse, they can have an 'insider' status. When, on the other hand, it is conducted by a psychologist, or sociologist, they may well not have insider status. Likewise, when research is carried on with, say, divorcees, being a divorcee may give you 'insider' status.

Comparative longitudinal and descriptive cross-sectional. These represent different approaches to practice and service evaluation. Many researchers have sought to evaluate services through the prespectives of those involved. This is most apparent in research on client or service-user experiences of interventions. Most often (but not always) these represent a single interview in which service users or clients report their views; these views form part of the text evaluating the services. Comparative longitudinal involves a comparison of two or more groups, using a longitudinal design. These enable change to be measured in relation to particular measures, and fall into (though not exclusively) the experimental and quasi-experimental tradition. We may wish to see the impact of counselling by health visitors on parenting. We would have a group who were counselled, another who were not, and we would compare the change or improvement in both groups in relation to their parenting.

Process and outcome evaluation. Outcome evaluation looks at the consequences of some intervention for particular groups in relation to particular goals. This may be, for example, whether depression is reduced, or a sense of empowerment is developed, or whether task competence improves. Process evaluation involves evaluating the processes that occur in practice. This, for example, can focus on the degree to which partnership was characteristic of client/practitioner relationships, or the extent to which a client and practitioner agreed on the nature and level of need.

Public and private accounts. Public accounts are those that participants are able, or prepared, to provide for researchers who perhaps interview them once or twice. These are, some researchers believe, limited, because people will be reluctant to provide deeper information without the building of a relationship. Hence, they think there will be a degree of superficiality in the findings. Some social scientists believe that the researcher needs to form a close relationship with participants in order to obtain the data 'truest' to the perspectives of those being researched. This comes with trust, even friendship. Others believe this is not necessary, particularly in areas of particular interest to the participant. They will be likely to talk of the most important facets of the issue, because it is one that exercises them. Even, for example, where interviewees are depressed, it is argued that they are frank about their lives in general, and the particular issues involved in the interview.

Immediate (micro) versus extended (macro) analysis. This is about the 'level' at which data collection and analysis occurs. Those who seek to examine matters that are, socially, close to participants tend to focus on micro considerations. What is the relationship between practitioner and client? What are the practices of information giving in a local health or social services office? Macro questions tend to look at the cultural and structural issues in society. Issues like inequality, gender relationships and racism, in particular how they are generated in society as a whole, and how they impact on the micro issues with which practitioners are generally concerned. Hence many of the issues about, for example, power or gender operate at the macro level. Some that focus on a micro level believe that macro level analysis is too general to provide the kinds of data that are useful and rigorous. Those of a macro disposition would argue that it is impossible to understand the micro situation without reference to the macro context.

Sealed versus open data collection. Experimental designs operate by seeking to minimize potential sources of 'contamination' of data. In evaluating an outcome, they identify a particular variable, generally intervention, and seek to show that this variable, and no other, is responsible for change, should it occur. This relates to the concerns about internal and external validity, which was discussed earlier in relation to randomized controlled trials. Others believe that, no matter how hard you try, it is simply not possible to 'seal off' a piece of research like that. There are always going to be influences lying outside the particular circumstance of the experiment, and these will always provide variables preventing attribution of cause to one defined element. Those people argue that society is an 'open system', that is a system of interactions that are impossible to seal off for research purposes.

Naturalism versus constructivism. These are positions taken up within qualitative social research, in particular ethnography. Those who espouse naturalism believe that the purpose of ethnography is to collect data in 'natural settings' presenting the reality of the situation in a way not possible with other methodologies. Hence the importance of direct observation. Those of a constructivist view may also be ethnographers, but believe that they are engaged in a process of 'constructing' a perspective on the situation – that is, one way to view that which is being observed. Indeed, they would also argue that those being studied are themselves engaging in constructs of their own situations, and acting on the basis of the constructs. Hence findings represent one perspective on the cumulative perspectives, or shared meanings, of those who are being studied.

Verstehen versus unproblematic interpretation. Verstehen refers to the act of achieving empathic understanding of the participants of a study. In order to write properly about a particular area of social life, you need to seek to see it 'through the eyes' of the participants themselves. In so doing you understand the meanings they ascribe to aspects of their social lives. Unproblematic interpretation, at the extreme opposite end of a continuum to verstehen, suggests that this is not necessary, and that apprehension of participants' views is not particularly problematic. Many view matters between these extremes, for example that complete immersion in meanings – complete empathy – is not possible, but that we should seek to gain maximum understanding. Others suggest that such meaning differences between researchers and researched are greatly exaggerated, while recognizing that there is some room for differences in meanings.

Service users' accounts: political empowerment versus critical approaches. Many of those studying service users take the view that research should be used to empower, and that therefore it is the responsibility of the researcher to present the views of users clearly as part of an evaluation. Indeed, involvement of service users in research design is also widely espoused. Research is an exercise in extending justice. Others see such views as far from unproblematic, and that the views of service users should be subject to critical appraisal. They are social actors just as any other participants in research, and their accounts should be as much a part of conventional research quality appraisal as any other element of the research. Users' views should not, therefore, simply be presented for evaluation purposes, but should be explained, and in turn themselves form part of the chain of explanation of the aspects of social life being studied. Such researchers argue that those who take a 'political-empowerment' approach are giving service users an epistemologically privileged position. That is they are not, in effect, subject to the same status as the rest of us in social life.

References

Atkinson, J.M. (1978) *Discovering Suicide*. London: Macmillan.

Baumrind, D. (1971) 'Current patterns of parental authority.' *Developmental Psychology Monographs 4*, 1–103.

Beck, A., Steer, R. and Garbin, M. (1988) 'Psychometric properties of the Beck Depression Inventory: Twenty five years of evaluation.' *Clinical Psychology Review 8*, 77–100.

Berg, B. (2000) *Qualitative Research Methods for the Social Sciences* (4th edn). Needham Heights, MA: Allyn and Bacon.

Bifulco, A. and Moran, P. (1999) *Wednesday's Child*. London: Routledge.

Black, T. (1999) *Doing Quantitative Research in the Social Sciences*. London: Sage.

Brewer, J. (1991) *Inside the RUC: Routine Policing in a Divided Society*. Oxford: Clarendon Press.

Bryman, A. (1988) *Quantity and Quality in Social Research*. London: Unwin Hyman.

Campbell, D. and Stanley, J. (1963) *Experimental and Quasi Experimental Designs for Research*. Chicago: Rand McNally.

Cheetham, J., Fuller, R., McIvor, G. and Petch, A. (1992) *Evaluating Social Work Effectiveness*. Buckingham: Open University Press.

Cigno, K. (1988) 'Consumer views of a family drop in centre.' *British Journal of Social Work 18*, 361–375.

Cigno, K. and Gore, J. (1999) 'A seamless service: Meeting the needs of children with disabilities through a multi agency approach.' *Child and Family Social Work 4*, 325–335.

Cormack, D. (ed) (2000) *The Research Process in Nursing*. Oxford: Blackwell Science.

Corney, R. (1984) *The Effectiveness of Attached Social Workers in the Management of Depressed Female Patients in General Practice*. Cambridge: Cambridge University Press.

Cornwell, J. (1984) *Hard-earned Lives: Accounts of Health and Illness from East London*. London: Tavistock.

Department of Health (1995) *The Challenge of Partnership in Child Protection*. London: The Stationery Office.

Doel, M. and Marsh, P. (1992) *Task-centred Social Work*. Aldershot: Ashgate.

Dowie, J. and Elstein, A. (eds) (1988) *Professional Judgement: A Reader in Clinical Decision Making*. Cambridge: Cambridge University Press.

Durkheim, E. (1952) *Suicide: A Study in Sociology*. Translated by John A. Spaulding and George Simpson; edited with an introduction by George Simpson. London: Routledge.

England, H. (1986) *Social Work as Art*. London: George Allen and Unwin.

Fawcett, B., Featherstone, B., Fook, J. and Rossiter, A. (2000) *Practice and Research in Social Work: Postmodern Feminist Perspectives*. London: Routledge.

Fells, J. and de Gruchy, S. (1991) 'Exploring the "need" for family centres: The perceptions of social workers and their importance for planning.' *British Journal of Social Work 21*, 173–184.

Ferrell, J. and Hamm, M.S. (eds) (1998) *Ethnography at the Edge: Crime, Deviance, and Field Research.* Boston, MA: Northeastern University Press.

Fisher, M. (1983) *Speaking of Clients.* Sheffield: University of Sheffield Press.

Fisher, M., Marsh, P. and Philips, D. (1986) *In and Out of Care: The Experiences of Children, Parents and Social Workers.* London: Batsford.

Geyman, J., Deyo, R. and Ramsey, S. (2000) *Evidence-based Clinical Practice: Concepts and Approaches.* Boston, MA: Butterworth-Heinemann.

Gibbons, J. with Thorpe, S. and Wilkinson, P. (1990) *Family Support and Prevention: Studies in Local Areas.* London: HMSO.

Gibbons, J., Conroy, S. and Bell, C. (1995) *Operating the Child Protection System: A Study of Child Protection Practices in English Local Authorities.* London: The Stationery Office.

Gillies, A. (2002) *Using Research in Nursing: A Workbook for Practitioners.* Abingdon: Radcliffe Medical.

Glaser, B. and Strauss, A. (1968) *The Discovery of Grounded Theory: Strategies for Qualitative Research.* London: Weidenfeld and Nicolson.

Goffman, E. (1961) *Asylums: Essays on the Social Situations of Mental Patients and Other Inmates.* Cambridge, MA: Harvard University Press.

Goldberg, E.M. and Wharburton, W. (1979) *Ends and Means in Social Work: The Development and Outcome of a Case Review System for Social Workers.* London: Allen and Unwin.

Hammersley, M. and Atkinson, P. (1995) *Ethnography: Principles in Practice.* London: Routledge.

Haralambos, M. and Holborn, M. (1991) *Sociology: Themes and Perspectives* (3rd edn). London: Collins.

Higgs, J. and Jones, M. (1995) *Clinical Reasoning in the Health Professions.* Oxford: Butterworth-Heinemann.

Howe, D. (1996) *Attachment and Loss in Child and Family Social Work.* Aldershot: Avebury.

Kuipers, E., Leff, J. and Lam, D. (2002) *Family Work for Schizophrenia: A Practical Guide.* London: Gaskell.

Leff, J. and Vaughn, C. (1985) *Expressed Emotion in Families: Its Significance for Mental Illness.* London: Guilford.

Maccoby, E. and Martin, J. (1983) 'Socialisation in the context of the family: Parent child interaction.' In M. Hetherington (ed) *Handbook of Child Psychology: Vol 4. Socialisation, Personality and Personal Development.* New York: Wiley.

Oppenheim, A.N. (1992) *Questionnaire Design, Interviewing and Attitude Measurement.* London: Printer Publishers.

Padgett, D. (1998) *Qualitative Methods in Social Work Research.* Thousand Oaks, CA: Sage.

Payne, M. (1993) *Linkages: Effective Networking in Social Care.* London: Whiting & Birch.

Pithouse, A. and Holland, S. (1999) 'Open Access family centres and their users: Positive results, some doubts and new departures.' *Children and Society 13*, 167–178.

Pithouse, A. and Lindell, S. (1994) 'Family care in the community: A case study of a family centre and its effectiveness in reducing abuse.' *Social Services Research 4*, 38–46.

Pithouse, A. and Lindell, S. (1996) 'Child protection services: Comparison of a referral family centre and a field social work service in South Wales.' *Research in Social Work 6*, 4, 473–491.

Pithouse, A., Holland, S. and Davey, D. (2001) 'Assessment in specialist referral family centre: Outcomes for children.' *Children and Society 15*, 302–314.

Ransford, H.E. (1968) 'Isolation, powerlessness and violence: A study of attitudes of participants in the Watts Riots.' *American Journal of Sociology 73*, 581–591.

Roberts, C. (1989) *Hereford and Worcester Probation Service Young Offender Project: First Evaluation Report.* Oxford: Department of Social and Administrative Studies, University of Oxford.

Rubin, A. and Babbie, E. (2001) *Research Methods for Social Work* (4th edn). Belmont, CA: Wadsworth/Thomson.

Sainsbury, E., Nixon, S. and Phillips, D. (1982) *Social Work in Focus: Clients and Social Workers' Perceptions of Long Term Social Work.* London: Routledge and Kegan Paul.

Schön, D. (1991) *The Reflective Practitioner* (2nd edn). Aldershot: Arena.

Schön, D. (1987) *Educating the Reflective Practitioner.* Oxford: Jossey-Bass.

Shaw, I. and Gould, N. (eds) (2001) *Qualitative Research in Social Work.* London: Sage.

Sheppard, M. (1990) *Mental Health: The Role of the Approved Social Worker.* Sheffield: Sheffield University Press.

Sheppard, M. (1991) *Mental Health Work in the Community: Theory and Practice in Social Work and Community Psychiatric Nursing.* London: Falmer.

Sheppard, M. (1995) 'Social work social science and practice wisdom.' *British Journal of Social Work 25*, 265–293.

Sheppard, M. (1996) 'Depression in the work of British health visitors: Clinical facets.' *Social Science and Medicine 43*, 11, 1637–1648.

Sheppard, M. (1997a) 'Depression in female health visitor consulters: Social and demographic factors.' *Journal of Advanced Nursing 26*, 921–929.

Sheppard, M. (1997b) 'Double jeopardy: The link between child abuse and maternal depression in child and family care social work.' *Child and Family Social Work 2*, 91–109.

Sheppard, M. (1997c) 'Social work practice in child and family care: A study of maternal depression.' *British Journal of Social Work 27*, 815–845.

Sheppard, M. (1998a) 'Practice validity, reflexivity and knowledge for social work.' *British Journal of Social Work 28*, 763–783.

Sheppard, M. (1998b) 'Social profile, maternal depression and welfare concerns in clients of health visitors and social workers.' *Children and Society 12*, 125–135.

Sheppard, M. (1999) 'Maternal depression in child and family care: The design, development and use of an instrument for research and practice.' In M. Ulas and A. Connor (eds) *Mental Health and Social Work.* London: Jessica Kingsley Publishers.

Sheppard, M. (2001) *Social Work Practice with Depressed Mothers in Child and Family Care.* London: The Stationery Office.

Sheppard, M. (2002) 'Depressed mothers' experience of partnership in child and family care.' *British Journal of Social Work 32*, 93–112.

Sheppard, M. (2004) *Prevention and Coping in Child and Family Care: Mothers in Adversity Coping with Child Care.* London: Jessica Kingsley Publishers.

Sheppard, M. and Ryan, K. (2003) 'Practitioners as rule using analysts.' *British Journal of Social Work 33*, 157–177.

Sheppard, M. and Watkins, M. (2000) 'The Parent Concerns Questionnaire: Evaluation of a self report instrument for the identification of problems and needs in child and family social work.' *Children and Society 14*, 194–206.

Sheppard, M., Newstead, S., Di Caccavo, A. and Ryan, K. (2001) 'Comparative hypothesis assessment and quasi triangulation as process knowledge assessment strategies in social work practice.' *British Journal of Social Work 31*, 863–885.

Sheppard, M., Newstead, S., Di Caccavo, A. and Ryan, K. (2000) 'Reflexivity and the development of process knowledge in social work: A classification and empirical study.' *British Journal of Social Work 30*, 465–488.

Silverman, D. (2000) *Doing Qualitative Research: A Practical Handbook.* London: Sage.

Smith, P. and Hunt, J. (1997) *Research Mindedness for Practice.* London: Churchill Livingstone.

Smith, T. (1996) *Family Centres and Bringing Up Children.* London: HMSO.

Social Care Institute for Excellence (SCIE) (2003) *Types and Quality of Knowledge in Social Care.* Bristol: The Policy Press.

Strauss, A. and Corbin, J. (1998) *Basics of Qualitative Research: Techniques and Procedures for Developing Grounded Theory.* Thousand Oaks, CA: Sage.

Takeuchi, D. (1974) *Grass in Hawaii: A Structural Constraints Approach.* MA thesis, University of Hawaii.

Tanner, C. and Lindeman, C. (1991) *Using Nursing Research.* New York: National League for Nursing.

Thompson, C. and Dowding, D. (2002) *Clinical Decision Making and Judgement in Nursing.* Edinburgh: Churchill Livingstone.

Vaughn, C. and Leff, J. (1976) 'The influence of family and social factors in the course of psychiatric illness: A comparison of schizophrenic and depressed neurotic patients.' *British Journal of Psychiatry 129*, 125–137.

Weppner, R. (ed) (1977) *Street Ethnography: Selected Studies of Crime and Drug Use in Natural Settings.* Beverly Hills, CA: Sage.

Subject Index

Author Index